LIVING IN WYOMING

SETTLING FOR MORE

TEXT BY SUSAN ANDERSON   PHOTOGRAPHY BY ZBIGNIEW BZDAK

ROCKRIDGE PRESS

Living in Wyoming
Settling for More

Published by Rockridge Press
6051 Margarido Drive
Oakland, California

Library of Congress Cataloging In Publication Data has been applied for

Designed by David Hurst
Edited by Peter Zimmerman
Printed in Hong Kong

ISBN 1-878867-05-9

PHOTOS: **page 2** Along the highway, south of Cody; **page 4** Cheyenne Frontier Days "Dandies"; **page 5** Crowheart; **page 8 (and front cover)** North 40 Lounge Rodeo, near Casper; **page 13** Fairy Falls Trail, Yellowstone National Park; **page 14** Along the Oregon Trail, near South Pass; **page 15 (and back cover)** Pathfinder Dam on the North Platte River; **page 16** Trailer park in Rock Springs; **page 17** Amoco Refinery, Casper; **page 18** Old Faithful, Yellowstone National Park; **page 19** Devils Tower National Monument; **page 154** Natrona County; **page 155** Rawlins; **page 157** Mammoth Hot Springs

ACKNOWLEDGMENTS

We would like to thank the Wyoming people who were so willing to talk with us and let us show their lives.

A grant from the Wyoming Council for the Humanities was a crucial boost, along with generous start-up donations from Dale Bohren, Linda Nix, John Barrasso, John and Jane Wold, Tom and Marta Stroock, Carol Fellows, Henry Louderbaugh, and Bill Schilling. US West and Sam Gappmayer of the Nicolaysen Art Museum made early commitments to the project, Lauren Bzdak designed an excellent promotional brochure, and the *Casper Star-Tribune* and KTWO Television granted time off for work on the book.

Wendy Curran, J.M. Neil, and Bart and Liz Rea were essential supporters at the beginning. Tobias Steed and Chris Burt brought the project to reality. In our travels, we were helped by Evelyn Miller and Jody Taylor, and hosted by Mike and Amy McClure, Fred Roberts, Ann Kreilkamp, Betty Stroock, John Carr, and Dennis and Wendy Curran. Wonderful story ideas came from Governor Mike and Jane Sullivan, Kate Dupont, Carolyn Paseneaux, Paul Krza, Geoff O'Gara, and helpful people working for many Wyoming businesses as well as federal and state agencies. Exum Mountain Guides and the National Outdoor Leadership School guided some of our outdoor adventures.

Linda Nix and Peter Zimmerman cast their discerning eyes on copy. We would also like to thank David Hurst for his imaginative work in designing the book, and Jon Schneeberger of *National Geographic* who generously critiqued the photos.

For our families—
Lauren, Dale, Danny and Hod

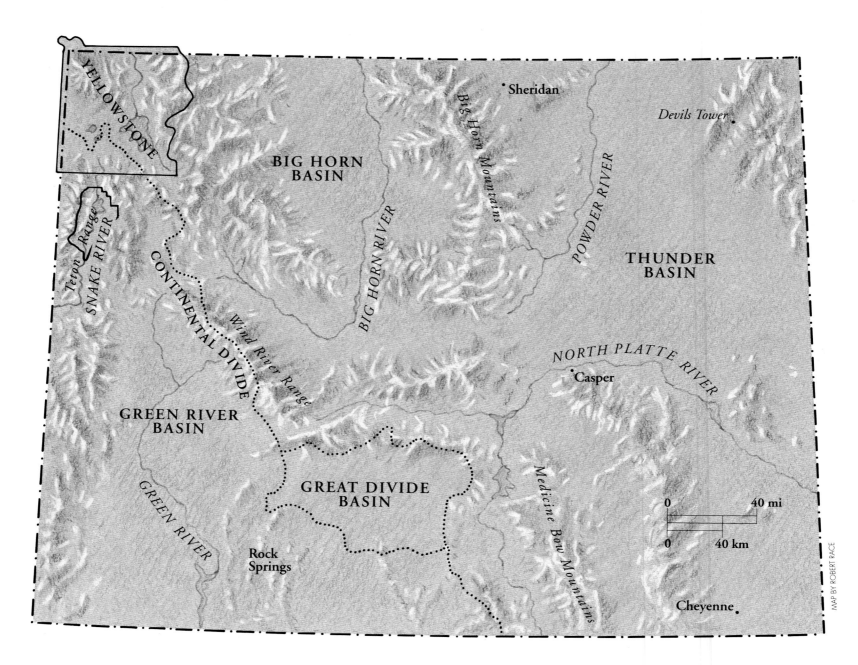

YELLOWSTONE

BIG HORN
BASIN

Sheridan

Devils Tower

Big Horn Mountains

Teton Range

SNAKE RIVER

CONTINENTAL DIVIDE

Wind River Range

BIG HORN RIVER

POWDER RIVER

THUNDER
BASIN

NORTH PLATTE RIVER

Casper

GREEN RIVER
BASIN

GREAT DIVIDE
BASIN

Medicine Bow Mountains

GREEN RIVER

Rock
Springs

0   40 mi

0   40 km

Cheyenne

MAP BY ROBERT RACE

PREFACE

When I was a newly transplanted television reporter in Wyoming, I would drive to cover news stories hundreds of miles across the state with photographer Zbigniew Bzdak. We'd argue for hours as the miles went by, debating what is good and bad about the state, and why neither of us wanted to live anywhere else.

By some standards, we were old-time residents by then—we'd each lived in Wyoming 10 years. Zbigniew came to Wyoming from Poland, via a long sojourn in South America. I followed a trail from Pittsburgh, New York, and San Francisco, before finding my home in Wyoming.

Zbigniew had "dreamt about traveling and taking pictures in exotic countries." Then he spent nine months photographing a kayak expedition on the Amazon River, from the source to the Atlantic Ocean. He says, "This trip gave me a whole new perspective on the world. Coming from jungle that is very vast, isolated, and exotic, I also found Wyoming to be vast, isolated, and exotic. I then started seriously thinking about documenting the uniqueness of Wyoming."

It was in front of a fireplace during a bitterly cold skiing trip in Yellowstone National Park that we decided to put our fascination with Wyoming into book form.

The basic question was simple—who chooses to live in the least populous state?

We looked for the answer 13,770 feet above sea level on the rocky summit of the Grand Teton, and 1,500 feet below ground in a huge, otherwordly trona mine. Our book focuses on people living contemporary lives in a harsh, but gorgeous environment.

As Zbigniew says, "I found Wyoming even more fascinating than I expected. I discovered the modern-day folklore: from the Indian powwow, to the Powder River Sheepherder's Fair, to an eccentric summer solstice celebration on Casper Mountain, to everyday ranching chores and 'old time' branding, which are all part of the culture here."

On this 20,000-mile journey of discovery, I was like a person in love—I wanted to know every little thing about the place and its people.

Where do all those pickups come from, at the only cafe in a town of 10? How do people feel about working underground all day, for about twice the average daily salary in the state?

What inspires someone to choose the job of a mountain guide? Now, I know some of the answers to these questions, and if anything, I'm more in love with Wyoming and its people than I was before.

—*Susan Anderson*

LIVING IN WYOMING

LIVING IN WYOMING

LIVING IN WYOMING

Francis Seely Webb leaned forward as she told me how her family came to Wyoming. The late newspaper editor was then 83, with a pale yellow-white bun of hair on top of her head.

"My father moved on down to Casper in the 1890s because, you know, he thought there were too many people in Deadwood," she said.

A mining boom had swelled Deadwood, South Dakota, to a population of 3,500.

People are always coming to Wyoming because it's too crowded in New York, Denver, or Deadwood. Fewer than 500,000 of them live on the vast land that makes up the least populous state. "Least populous. . . Is that unpopular?" asked a road crew member eating hamburgers at the Waltman Cafe.

Not to me. When Wyoming dropped to last in population, below Alaska, in 1985, I was happy. I was pleased with myself for doing what 230 million United States residents hadn't done. I moved to Wyoming.

I made my decision while lost in thought, standing in hip boots in the middle of a stream, holding a fishing pole on the Vee Bar Ranch near Centennial. The sound of the flowing water, the physical yearning for a tug on the line, the total focus of my eyes on the point just under the water surface where I might see a trout, produced a hypnotic state so powerful that I didn't notice the arrival of twelve cattle who were standing on the stream bank when I turned around. I'd blended into the natural scene so much that the cattle weren't bothered by me. When they did see me, most of them kept munching. A couple looked up, and paused, with light green grass blades hanging from their wet, white mouths. I didn't move, they didn't either. We watched each other for a serene moment. It was not something I had felt ever before, anywhere else, in a busy American life.

Where there aren't enough people, you prize the ones you've got, as if they were each long-awaited only children. That attitude brings surprising rewards for people who've been traditionally undervalued.

Women got the right to vote in Wyoming before anyone else in the country, mostly because state officials were worried about a declining population. That was in 1869, when half of the Wyoming Territory's 18,000 residents left in one year after work on the transcontinental railroad was finished. The idea was that giving women the vote might convince some of the Civil War widows and orphans in the East to move west. At that time, men outnumbered women seven to one. The radical decision to share the vote had its detractors. One opposing politician named W.R. Steele informed the territorial legislature, "Woman can't engage in politics without losin' her virtue. No woman ain't got the right to sit on a jury, nohow, unless she is a man and every lawyer knows it."

The numbers are still extreme. Numerically, each person in Wyoming has a one-in-225,000 chance of becoming a U.S. Senator.

In California, the odds are one in 12 million. Wyoming's 450,000 people get two senators and California's 24 million get two. Being a senator from a state with only enough people to make a medium-sized city has its humbling aspects. Wyoming Sen. Alan Simpson says, "You go home, and half the people on the street know you, and *all* of them feel perfectly fine about saying 'Hey Al, what about my retirement check?'"

Governor Mike Sullivan is listed in the Cheyenne phone book. Late one night he received a phone call from someone who identified himself as Byron. He was in the city jail, and didn't like the food. Governor Sullivan referred Byron to the mayor of Cheyenne, who was in the phone book, too. And the mayor also heard from Byron.

Dubois is a town small enough that a candidate for mayor was able to buy all the copies of the newspaper the day it ran a story about his shoplifting conviction (200 copies). His opponent persuaded the publisher to re-print, then himself bought all the copies and distributed them door to door. The mayor lost.

The one statewide newspaper, the *Casper Star-Tribune*, has a policy to print all the letters it receives. Each day, two to four pages are full of snide attacks on Sen. Simpson (and often his lengthy, detailed half-page replies), personal remarks to other frequent letter-writers, thanks to the hospital for saving a life, complaints about potholes. Topics such as how the roads are plowed in snowstorms and who gets refunds for cancelled rock concerts can be debated for weeks. The letters are petty and avidly read by subscribers curious to see what their neighbors are up to now. Wyoming is a small town stretched over a big state. It covers about the same square mileage as New England, with one of its 23 counties alone the size of Connecticut.

There are five people per square mile. Several thousand people live on my square mile in Casper, so there are thousands of miles in the state with no people at all. None. This oddball population situation has produced a lot of people who think they can do anything, and not much competition to stop them.

They begin a business or a new project, on the conviction that there's no harm in trying. And a high number of start-up ventures fail, victims of the too-small markets and economies of scale that are the flip side of a low population.

"This is a great place for the isolated thinker," says Ann Kreilkamp, an astrologer and philosopher who lives in a canvas structure called a yurt at the foot of the Tetons. "Ideas seed themselves in the mountains," she says. "It's easier to have your own voice because it's not rubbed against so many others."

Uncrowding is a major theme of life in the remote West. The other is living with, or trying to tame, the wild land. If you subtract service industries, much of the major work done in the state relates to the land: minerals extraction and production, outdoor tourism, recreation, wildlife and land management, farming, and ranching.

In a role even more striking than providing livelihood, land sets a mood that works powerfully on the spirit. Says Kreilkamp, "Nature is more prevalent than culture. When winter is here, nature is the predominant theme. The artificial is overshadowed."

In James Michener's "Centennial," a woman traveling along the Oregon Trail in Wyoming says, "We both thought that if we were to live within the shadow of such majestic hills, we would become like them. . . . I feel assured that any family that grows up in such novel surroundings will be strong and different."

Living the outdoor life is a major reason people choose to live where they will earn below the national average in almost every field. "Add $15,000 for the view," says one of my employers. And another $10,000 for the fishing. In Wyoming, more people fish each year than ride a bus or fly in an airplane.

Seventy-five percent of the people live within two hours of a ski slope. All live near big-game hunting areas and within hours of the largest antelope herd in North America, some of the last bison, a large elk herd, and enough grizzly bears to maul several people in some years. There are twice as many sheep as people, and a few thousand more mule deer. Driving the 100 miles from Shoshoni to Casper one evening, I counted 212 antelope and 48 cars. That's about average for that drive.

You can spend a year in Mexico and speak no Spanish. People grow up in Washington, D.C., without ever visiting the White House. And you can live in Wyoming without being touched by the surroundings. A teenager in the 45,000-person town of Casper can watch MTV, go to the mall, see Bon Jovi at the Events Center, work at Burger King, drive a Miata, and live the same life as a cousin in Mamaroneck, Chicago or Atlanta.

But this book introduces people who live in the Wyoming described by its Indian name, a place of "mountains and valleys alternating." They are like the herd of longhorns who, abandoned for dead in a nineteenth century Wyoming winter, survived until spring and became a breed uniquely suited to the cold weather. They are people who weather winter and isolation because they believe where they are is the heart of somewhere, in the middle of other people's nowhere.

LIVING IN WYOMING

INVENTING A BUSINESS

There are traditional ways of making a living in Wyoming, mostly tied to the land. There are nerve-wracking ways of making a living by riding the energy and mining roller coasters. But the oldest way is also newly popular: inventing a business. From mountain man Jim Bridger's successful little trade selling oil from a seep near Casper to Oregon Trail travelers needing axle grease, to Christen Industries of Afton, makers of aerobatic biplanes for export all over the country, Wyoming businesses have not relied on huge built-in markets. Instead, they've had to be creative.

"Guns are male jewelry," says inventor Dick Casull, to explain the love of good weapons. He designed his first gun from a car tailpipe when he was a boy. Now he is the inventor of the world's most powerful handgun, the Casull. It's just one of his designs for the Freedom Arms Factory in the town of Freedom. He says the business is based in Wyoming because of low taxes and a positive attitude toward guns.

"The snake is under my control," says Lewis Ray of his rattler. It's one of about a dozen in cages at his taxidermy shop in Casper, where he once kept rattlesnakes as guards in his gun case. The sign above his shop door reads, "Moose or Mouse, Bring it to our House." Taxidermists consider restoring an animal's carcass to a lifelike state to be an art. Ray imports glass eyes from Europe because of their craftsmanship. "You have to know anatomy," he says, "where to put the ears and how they set."

The man who bosses the 2,500 animals used in Cheyenne Frontier Days is a 5'2",
130-pound perfect example of what people think a cowboy looks like. He's even
bowlegged. Don Kensinger has "helped out" with the world's largest rodeo for 42
years, volunteering his hours to shop for horses in Mexico, organize the animals
and run the show. In his spare time, he and his wife manage the Taco John chain,
which they own. The Disney corporation has hired him as a "rodeo consultant"
to set up their western theme park in Paris.

A FAX machine and computer with modem can do wonders for a business based in a renovated chicken coop 27 miles from the nearest town (Dubois, pop. 900). Equitour sent a thousand people on exotic horse trips in 19 countries in 1989—all from the Bitterroot Ranch, and all with the aid of modern technology, and old-fashioned sense about horses and people.

Equitour's brochure of horse trips tells you on the cover how to reach the company by telex, FAX, and an international 800 number. The company's founder, Bayard Fox, works from a tiny structure that once housed hens, but now features instant access to travel agents all over the world. He sits in his office, in heavily mudded rubber boots, rough jacket and cowboy hat, reading a FAX just arrived from Argentina. The view from his window is of a storm coming in over the Absaroka mountains. His 600-acre ranch is bounded by national forest, the Wind River Indian Reservation, and a designated wilderness area. The east fork of the Wind River gives the land a strip of greenery and trees that follows its banks.

"It's very inspiring to sit here and work," says Bayard. "I knew I wanted an international business, but it wouldn't have been possible just 15 years ago. I would have had to live on Park Avenue to have a business like this. Technology lets us set up here as well as anywhere else. Nobody does any business off the street these days, except selling hot dogs."

When Bayard bought the Bitterroot Ranch in 1971, after retiring from the CIA, things were different. He was guiding hunting trips near Dubois and raising horses. But he got a lucky break in the first year, when an exhausted French journalist looking for a relaxing assignment came to visit. The story that was published led to a steady stream of French visitors in the early years. "A cowboy who speaks French, they love it," says Bayard, who speaks seven languages from his time with the government.

Eight years later, a young woman whose family had lost its ranch at the foot of Mt. Kilimanjaro in Tanzania came to help care for the horses. "She was the best hand I ever had," Bayard says of Mel. "And being no fool, I married her." She still cares for the horses, but has also acquired an astonishing collection of animals.

"It's very inspiring to sit here and work," says Bayard Fox in his tiny office at the edge of a national forest and the Wind River Indian Reservation. He runs Equitour riding holidays from a converted chicken house on his Bitterroot Ranch.

"I grew up in Kenya, so teeming with wildlife," she says. "This was wild and empty, kind of lonely." So she began adding animals. "These are my friends."

Here's the latest count:

6 cats
4 dogs
20 Barbados sheep
11 peacocks
5 geese
40 ducks
16 guinea fowl
20 turkeys
15 cows
124 horses

One fierce small cat was brought to Wyoming from Kenya after it hissed and alerted Mel to the fact that a spitting cobra was also in the tent. These particular cobras can stand up to a height of six feet and paralyze a victim with spit. Mel was able to clear out of the snake's way because of the kitten's warning. The kitten had already had an exciting life—its mother had been strangled by a boa constrictor.

Mules are history at the Bitterroot. One winter when the ranch was snowed in from Thanksgiving until March, a mule broke into the barn and ate the dog food. Bayard killed the mule and fed it to the dogs. Now just the dogs and peacocks eat the dog food.

Over time, the Foxes have built 16 cabins and they can handle 28 guests with a staff of 20 in the summer. The first tour this year is a group of Australians. The Foxes also guide two international trips a year, including a demanding horseback tour of game reserve land in Kenya. Their nine-year-old son goes with them on the tours, stopping in Paris and London on the way, before returning to his Wyoming life, where he catches the school bus several miles down a rutted dirt road from the Foxes' house.

"It's odd to have a million-dollar ranch and no cash because the horses have to eat," says Bayard of the years when they heated only with wood. They're finally building their first addition that will allow their son to move his bed out of the middle of the living room.

The business of booking people on horse tours throughout the world is booming. But the Foxes don't want to expand what they offer on their own ranch, a tour of "The Outlaw Trail" and a "Pony Express Ride."

"I have no desire to get rich as long as I can live like this," says Bayard. "I like the wide-open spaces. That, to me, is the most precious thing about this place."

"They make it not so lonely," says Mel Fox of the exotic and domestic animals she keeps on the Bitterroot Ranch. Before settling in Wyoming, she was a park ranger in East Africa, her homeland. One horse tour she leads in Wyoming traces the Pony Express Route for six hours of hard riding a day. "Riding is a psychological thing," says Mel. "Bravery is an issue."

The reason one of the largest airplane charter companies in the country is based in Greybull is "not tax advantages so much as air space and breathing space," according to co-owner Gene Powers. A bad-boy independence is part of not only his style but also his fondness for Wyoming. He likes to ride his motorcycle around the airstrip, which is perched on a striking red bluff overlooking this town of just over 2,000 people in the state's Big Horn Basin.

His painters are working out in the open air on the runway. The extra military planes bought by the company and awaiting refurbishing are casually parked out in a field. And Gene can jump in his plane on the spur of the moment and take off, which he did with photographer Zbigniew Bzdak. No flight plan, no consultation with anyone but himself. He doesn't ask permission for much.

"I'd get thrown in jail for that little ride in a big city," he says. And he knows what he has in Wyoming is unique because, as he points out, "You can't ride a motorcycle on the runway even in goddamn Billings, Montana."

The five-million-dollar business of Hawkins and Powers Aviation buys old military planes and helicopters, adapts them for other uses, and rents them out. Fire fighting is the bread and butter of the operation, but there is also a glamorous sideline supplying vintage planes for movies.

"That one was in 'Always,'" says Gene of a silver plane that could double for the one that took Ilsa to Lisbon in the last scene of "Casablanca." The office of Hawkins and Powers is itself like a movie set—a handsome crew of six British filmmakers stomps through, two oil-stained mechanics come in for coffee, and a constant repartee goes on between the women in the office and the pilots. The company employs 90 people, which makes it big business in Greybull.

But Gene Powers doesn't act like an important businessman. When did he buy the company?

"Aw, I don't know. Ask Jan (the office manager)." He and Dan Hawkins bought out their boss in 1969 when there were six planes, three helicopters, and 12 employees.

"You can't ride a motorcycle on the runway even in goddamn Billings, Montana," says Gene Powers. But he does what he wants at the airport near Greybull that's dominated by Hawkins and Powers Aviation. The five-million-dollar business buys old military airplanes and re-tools them for rental to fire fighters and moviemakers.

They've grown into one of the largest charter fire fighting outfits in the country, but Gene likes to downplay his success.

"I've really come up in the world," he says. "In 1944, I was a young, healthy guy in a new privateer (a classic Navy bomber). Now I'm an old fart in a broken-down plane." But Gene says museums "would drool" for this particular broken-down plane. It's one of the six remaining C119's in the world—and Gene owns five of them.

"I don't know where you would find a 1944 anything that's still appropriate, efficient, and competitive," he says of the one-time war plane that now bombs forest fires.

Gene has been flying for 48 of his 62 years, ever since he ran away from home to live at the Sheridan airport when he was 13. The owner said he could camp out in the hangar on one condition: he had to keep going to eighth grade. Gene had already "terrorized the neighborhood," he says, with a Model A Ford he had built "from a pile of junk" at age 12. When Gene was 16, his two older brothers were flying in World War Two for the Army, and he was "left home farming."

"I got tired of looking at horses' behinds while the others were off flying," he says. So he altered his birth certificate and joined the Navy to fly in the war.

It's not simply love of flying that explains Gene Powers. He loves the planes themselves. He has a degree in aeronautical engineering, and over the years he's modified nearly every plane he's owned, making him "some kind of engineering genius," according to an admiring office worker. For example, a pilot making a hair-raisingly low sweep over a forest fire in a Hawkins and Powers Privateer has Gene to thank for the reassuring third jet he decided to install on top of the plane. The extra jet could make the difference between crashing into the flames, or lifting up over them.

"It gives an extra push to get out of a tough situation," says Gene. His current goal is "to build the best air tanker in the world. I want to put jet engines on the Neptune and a new drop system." Then he wants to "go to Mexico and chase women."

Provided he can ride his motorcycle on the runway.

People coming upon Hawkins and Powers Aviation are startled to see dozens of World War II fighter planes lined up neatly on the runway. Company owners say "breathing space" is what keeps one of the country's largest aviation charter companies located in an isolated part of Big Horn County.

What kind of person would buy a silk braid cord, carefully unwind each strand, press it, then rewind it to match the trim on a wedding dress worn in 1914? A very patient one, who thinks working with the left-behind objects of bygone days is important.

Kay-Karol Horse Capture, one of the Rocky Mountain region's few trained conservators, came from the Chicago art world to the small town of Cody (pop. 6,500) to restore treasures in the Buffalo Bill Historical Center. And she's found disciples in her basement room, where volunteers huddle over magnifying lights to do their rescue work.

Twelve of them slaved over the wedding dress, once worn by Buffalo Bill's daughter, Arta. The dress is now the star attraction in a room that features elegant trappings of Buffalo Bill's lifestyle in the days when his Wild West Show made him "more famous than the President," according to a newspaper clipping from that era.

When the gorgeous ivory silk moire taffeta dress came to Kay-Karol, it was missing a cuff, lapel, and collar. What wasn't missing was falling apart . . . "a two-dimensional nightmare," she says. Imagining how young Arta held her classic frame (waist size: 21 inches) was the first step in recreating the look of wealthy Western life. Next came a month of studying and stitching.

"It's the business of saving something," Kay-Karol says. "There's something healing about it, also something very rewarding about working on an article and saying, 'My God, it was falling apart, and suddenly we have a piece that will last a hundred years longer.'"

Outside of Cody is Old Trail Town, Bob and Terry Edgar's dream-come-true. Over 13 years, they have hauled 26 abandoned historical buildings to their land, including a cabin used by Butch Cassidy and the oldest remaining saloon in northwest Wyoming, its door still pocked with bullet holes. They've expanded to include a graveyard of western characters, such as Jeremiah Johnson, relocated from his original burial site in Southern California.

Bruce and Adam Stamper find work in Dubois shaving logs for a house made of giant spruce trees. Independent logger John Jeffs hired log cabin specialist Callum Mackay, a Scottish mountain climbing immigrant, to build his dream house. Swedish tie hacks helped settle the area, and giant wood burls or logs are a major feature of old and new construction.

John Mionczynski's business is goats and their pack saddles. He sells the saddles internationally, and conducts pack trips in rough mountainous areas. He says goats can go where no other pack animal can and they "provide pleasant company on the trail." He raises and breeds the animals on his land just above the old mining town of Atlantic City.

When the summer heat dries up pasture land, ranchers move their sheep and cattle to higher ground. For more than a hundred years every June, the dusty Arminto Stock Trail and the 33 Mile Trail in Natrona County have been crowded with a traffic jam of animals, passing places with names like "First Water," "Fifty Mile Flat," and "Lone Bear Road."

WORKING THE LAND

The land in Wyoming impacts more than eyes and imagination. It's the base for the state's most beloved ways of working—ranching and farming.

As a job-style, agriculture offers some impressive contrasts. A sheep-and-cattle outfit in Natrona County run by the Ellis family sets a standard for being modern. The boys carefully plan their cattle drive up the historic Arminto stock trail to summer pasture so they can stop each afternoon at 5. That schedule is not dictated by watering holes, tired animals, or even a desire to eat dinner. No, 5 p.m. is when the game show "Jeopardy" can be picked up on the TV in their traveling trailer home, and they don't intend to miss it. In the same county, you can find another old-time family, on the Taylor ranch, branding cattle in the most old-fashioned way possible. They bring in some neighbors, lasso the cattle, wrestle them down, and mark them with a brand heated over a wood fire in the field. Back at the Ellis ranch, the cattle are pinned down on a table that takes most of the bruises, and fun, out of the process.

What these families share is a several-generation history of raising the crops and the animals, dominated by seasons, weather, and the government, which owns half of the land in the state, and is a force to be reckoned with for those who use public land.

Skip Forbes is moving sheep and looking for a stray dog. "You need an old dog to make up for the mistakes of the others," he says. His six-month-old pup took off when some lambs "got excited" crossing a stream.

Brandings are both a necessity and a good reason to socialize in spring. Friends are invited to the Taylor Ranch to help in the dusty, bruising job of getting the calves to the ground, where they're castrated and branded, while the cows gather noisily outside the corral, mooing for their calves.

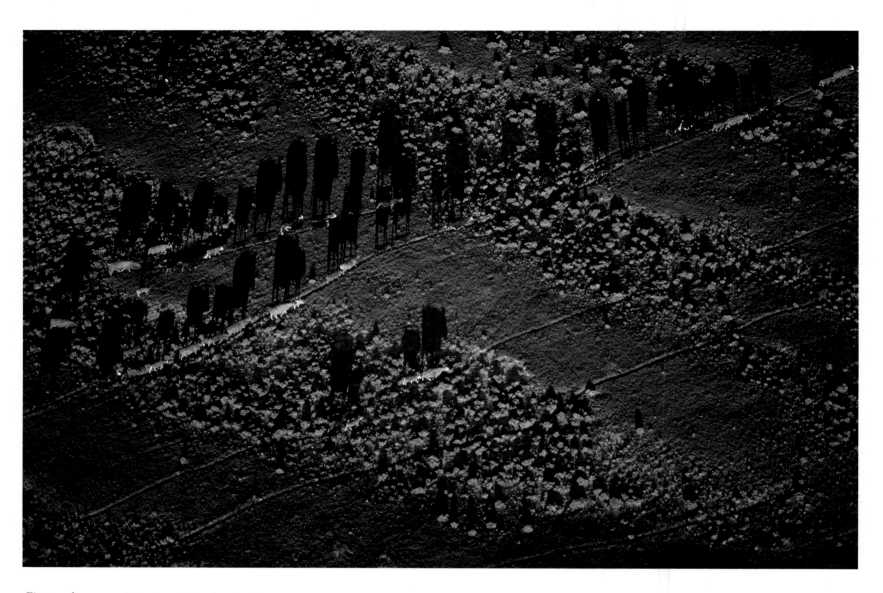

First cattle came to Wyoming. Then sheepherders tried to fence the land. Fights over the land and stealing of animals have been bitter throughout the state's history, climaxing in the 1892 Johnson County War.

Branding at the Taylor Ranch on a hot dusty day in May

Juan and Francisco come from the same small town in Mexico, but I met them in a sheep camp in western Wyoming. I was only the sixth person they had seen in the months when they moved the herd to high summer pasture. They hadn't been back to Mexico for almost two years, but Francisco had plenty of mementos, stored in a metal box at the head of his cot.

"My daughter's confirmation," he says, showing me a color picture of frowning teenagers dressed in white.

He is 31 and has been home four times in nine years of herding sheep in Wyoming. He has managed to father three more children in that time, to make a total of six. The box also holds a stack of romantic cards from his wife. One showed a couple walking on a beach at sunset, surrounded by hearts of pink, purple and red, then a love poem curved around the hearts. "For my husband," she wrote, in Spanish. He was proud of the card. Next, he pulled a rifle out from under his bed. He's been trying to get it to work, since his boss told him he couldn't take pistols into the bars anymore.

Fred Roberts is the rancher who employs the two, and 14 other sheepherding aliens. Every two weeks he makes the long trip by horse to bring supplies for the camp, well above 10,000 feet in the Greys River area of western Wyoming. His friend Steve, a computer programmer from Salt Lake City, is with him. For the eighth year, Steve is spending a week of his vacation in August, riding horses in the Wyoming Range with Fred. The two of them, photographer Zbigniew Bzdak, and I leave our trucks at what already seemed like the top of the mountain. We got on horses Francisco had brought for us, and followed single-file up through pastures beginning to show a warm autumn mix of green, orange, and yellow.

The tent is under a strip of trees on top of a ridge that drops off steeply in two directions. To the west, even higher mountains rise up beyond the canyon and stand between this range and Utah.

Francisco Guerrerro and Juan Torres leave their families in Mexico for years at a time for the opportunity to make better money herding sheep in western Wyoming. Their primitive camp is moved every few days to keep the sheep moving through their mountainous summer range at a chilly 10,000 feet above sea level.

The first job at the summer camp is to count the sheep. How many have been killed by coyotes and the bear that's been reported in the area, how many have died from being old, young, or weak.

"He's got a good count," says Fred. "Twelve hundred ewes, 800 lambs." To wrangle the 2,000 animals into one place to be counted, one horseman and three dogs chase the sheep into something like a single-file line. The dogs are very good. They do what has to be done to outsmart the sheep. The ewes leap as they run sometimes. They look like the nursery-rhyme cow jumping over the moon. Low sheep voices fill our ears. A few notes higher are the barking dogs. And at the top of the register are trillings from the Mexicans as they talk to the sheep in Spanish.

Fred and Steve leave to visit another camp. We look around, and sniff the thin air. It's harder to breathe at this elevation, but each breath is dense with tree and grass smells. Then woodsmoke drifts into the nose, followed by a harsher scent of sheep and horses. The worst smells are inside the 15-year-old tent that Juan packs up every two days to move to new pasture. It has two cots, a metal box for cooking fires, and a smell of unrefrigerated food, lard just short of rancid. And rough jerky with animal hair still stuck to it.

Juan does the cooking, and his tortillas taste wonderful. The coffee is cooked camp-style, grounds dumped into a pot that sits on the stove for hours. It feels like it leaves a thick coating on the teeth. I hate to think what happens in my stomach.

Four working sheepdogs lie about the camp, acting as if they know their importance as business partners. Fred forgot to bring food for them, so Francisco goes off to slaughter a lamb for the dogs—handing them raw, bloody meat minutes after slicing the lamb's throat. They collapse and sleep for the rest of the afternoon. The gutted, dripping lamb carcass is hung from a tree about six feet from the tent.

"My brother came here first," says Francisco, when we join the dogs in sitting around idly. "But he died." This is the ninth year Francisco has worked for Fred, earning $7,200 a year. It's a huge amount of money in Mexico, and Francisco sends some of it home to his family.

"But not all," he says. With the rest, he hopes to find a girlfriend. He says he needs one, maybe two. There will be more chance for that when they take the sheep to their winter range in the Red Desert near Rock Springs. His looks must be an asset. He is as slim as his mustache, dark and smiling, with a very warm, white smile. And he walks, not like a cowboy, but like a gaucho, the elite graceful horsemen of South America.

"What about your wife?" asks Zbigniew. "She is for taking care of children," replies Francisco. His partner, Juan, is more shy, and not married. Both say in their home town of Atlixtac there is no work. But living the way they do is lonely. "I often just sit in the tent and feel sad," says Juan.

Later, as it gets dark, Zbigniew and Francisco spend an hour and a half talking about food. It starts with a discussion of how to make ceviche. They agree the raw white fish needs onion and cilantro. But the merits of lime compared to lemon require detailed discussion, which occupies the slow time it takes for the sky to turn from rose to deep blue. Francisco begins to describe the fruits that grow near his town, lingering wistfully on mangoes. And he says how hard it is for him to get used to the Wyoming cold.

"It's almost as if they sacrifice their lives for the people at home," says Zbigniew.

After dark, the dogs begin barking fiercely, and two sheepherders who work for a Mormon rancher from Utah ride up. Two important members of their crew have disappeared—the Great Pyrenees guard dogs. They are trained to live with sheep. The men say the dogs think they *are* sheep. They're covered with stringy white fur and look like sheep. In the canine social arrangement, guard dogs are separate from herding dogs. The two kinds don't even eat together. The Pyrenees eat with the ewes and lambs.

The newcomers are Peruvian Mormons, converted by a missionary last year. Oscar has been here only a week, a refugee from the political unrest in his country. But he, too, is lonely. "My children—two and four," is all he says.

Now the conversation turns to religion. "Fred's religion is money," says Francisco, and they laugh. The Mormons have a newer tent, a nicer stove, and caffeine-free Coke. The next day, they find their guard dogs with Francisco's herd. Oscar can only get them to come with him by lassoing one. It wouldn't do to lose them. In addition to the coyotes and bears they guard against, there's their price—one thousand dollars, ten weeks' salary for a sheepherder.

The Peruvians saw two lambs killed by a bear a day ago, and they keep a fire going all night at their camp on the next hill. But Francisco laughs about "El Oso," the bear. He is kind enough to allow us to share the tent, just wide enough for two of us to squeeze on the floor between the cots. Backpackers in this kind of country worry about a bit of bacon grease on their sleeping bags. But we laid down a few feet from a pool of blood under the lamb carcass. To say I slept would be a lie. Dogs barked throughout the night, and they may be the reason "El Oso" didn't come to our camp.

In a lull of barking, we heard one ewe bawling in the night. "She looks for her lamb," says Francisco. The dead lamb. In the morning, she was still calling.

The living conditions are primitive—a tent (with holes), two cots, and a wood burning stove. In the division of camp duties, Francisco supervises the sheep and Juan does the cooking.

Sheepdogs are crucial working partners for two men herding two thousand animals. When the dog food ran out, Francisco slaughtered a ewe, tossing the heart to a dog, before slinging the carcass over his horse and returning to camp.

Jody Taylor lives on one of the historic Hole-in-the-Wall ranches, and says of the area sheep men, "They got their own way of ranching—houses and life in town and ranching in the country." He flies a small plane to check on his herds, cutting down on the need for hired help.

Jeff Jarrard and his brother Justin have invested in their own small sheep herd. They both went to Natrona County High School in Casper, but their lives are quite different from the teens who cruise CY Avenue on weekends—they're on the range with the sheep during the summer. Their dad, Roy, says "you don't have to have a fancy house to have a happy family."

Taking a break for supper, teenagers Justin Jarrard and Aaron Raley say they don't get lonely on the stock trail—they're too busy. "JJ" saw a snake near the sheep and "took care of him. I hit him on the head with a rock."

It's hot, dirty work at a branding, and Jolene Pike doesn't fight very hard to avoid a dunking at the end of the day.

A modern ranching outfit owned by Pinky Ellis travels in a comfortable mobile home, the horses tied to the back for use when needed to keep stray animals together. These cowboys break every day at five o'clock to watch television. A neighboring rancher says cows move faster than sheep, but "they all move faster than Pinky's animals."

MINING THE LAND

Wyoming's favorite symbols come from ranching, but mining pays the bills. Ten times as many people get paychecks from minerals companies as from agriculture . . . and they're good paychecks.

A coal miner makes over $30,000 a year in Wyoming. In an old song, Tennessee Ernie Ford sings about a coal miner loading "16 tons." Back then, this sounded like a lot. But Jean Kirking, a coal miner at the AMAX Eagle Butte Mine near Gillette, laughs at 16 tons. Her truck lifts 190 tons in one load. Coal mining in the rich Powder River Basin broke production records year after year in the eighties, while the work force got smaller. That's because the business of mining gets more technical every day. A degree in computer science is more helpful now than a strong back.

In Gillette, one fifth of the population works in coal mines, making Wyoming tied for first place in coal production in the United States. Mining is "a thinking man's job," according to AMAX Coal executive Ron Spangler. Miners earn an average of $17 per hour operating technical equipment, often monitored by computer. Being a truck driver in the open pit mines means driving trucks of 190- to 240-ton capacity. Twenty percent of the mine truck drivers are women.

One of the hardest and best paid jobs is operating the steam shovel, which is powered by 4,160-volt cables pulled along behind. Digging the ore, then transferring it to a waiting truck is a delicate operation, performed on a 200-ton load.

The Powder River Basin of north central Wyoming contains the largest coal deposit in the world. At one time, the 65- by 100-mile area was an inland sea. In 1988, 136-million tons of coal were produced in Campbell County.

Trona miners make good money, but their workplace is another world: dusty, dark, and potentially dangerous. A day underground, and you see why the companies pay over $40,000 a year to get people skilled enough to handle the job and willing to tough it out 1,500 feet below ground.

You don't just go down into an FMC trona mine in Sweetwater County. First, management puts you in a reasonable state of fear during two hours of safety training.

FMC officials are proud of the mine's safety record, which compares "very favorably" to the national average for underground mines. The list of precautionary measures is long—and scary to a novice. First on the list is fire.

A small amount of methane is released by oil shale under the trona bed, so fire could be a danger. No smoking is allowed in the mine, which explains the popularity of chewing tobacco among the miners—in the vending machines at the mine shaft entrance, tobacco tins fill three of the slots, next to the candy and gum. Because a camera's flash is hot, it's a potential fire hazard. Our escort tested the methane level in each location before pictures could be taken.

Each person going into the mine carries a self-rescue system—an eight-pound strap-on affair resembling a gas mask. The system converts the killing carbon monoxide of a fire into carbon dioxide for you to breathe—although FMC officials say a fire serious enough to require the self-rescue equipment has never happened in the mine's 42-year history. In the process of converting carbon monoxide into carbon dioxide, the system's mouthpiece heats up. (Our guide at the FMC mine, Tim Hilderman, survived a serious mine fire in Arizona where he had the presence of mind to keep breathing through the mouthpiece while his lips burned and his esophagus was blistered. But he says people have yanked off the masks and died, so a blistered throat seems a small price to pay.)

Visitors are urged to stay under the areas where the tunnel roof has been reinforced with metal bolts. Millions of dollars and many employee hours are spent making the roof stable. Bits of rock can fall out of the wall or ceiling, which is why hard hats are required. We're warned to avoid the 4,160-volt cables that drive the huge mining machines. Only people wearing electrical linemen's gloves touch those.

Trona miners operate huge machines that carry 180 tons in one load. This shuttle car with ore will dump its load on a conveyor belt 1,500 feet under western Wyoming. The ore is processed to make baking soda—nearly five million tons of ore a year from this mine owned by the FMC Corporation.

The FMC mine near Green River is the fifth largest underground mine of any kind in the country. To get to it, you ride a cage that is lowered slowly down below older and older layers of earth to the trona bed. Fifty million years ago, there was a huge trapped lake in western Wyoming, like the Great Salt Lake. Because water didn't flow out, rich plant and animal deposits were left, which formed the largest seam of trona in the world. When trona is processed, it forms soda ash, which is used to make glass and baking soda.

On the way down, there's the sound of fans blowing 1.5 million cubic feet per minute of fresh air into the mine. At the bottom, for the first 30 feet, it's like walking into a huge wine cellar. But rapidly the tunnels narrow to a size so small we occasionally must duck while riding in a jeep to avoid mineral deposits, bolts, and other objects hanging from the ceiling. "There are more miles of road in this mine than in the city of San Francisco," says Tim, as he brings the jeep to a stop at the sight of an oncoming light. We detour into a side tunnel, watch the other vehicle loom out of darkness, then disappear again into total blackness. Vehicles leaving the mine have the right-of-way.

Walking in the tunnels takes concentration. Because of the dark, you don't have any side vision, just the circle lit up by your miner's light. If someone walks toward you and you look directly at them, the powerful light on your hat hits their eyes; you're supposed to tilt your head up or down when you look at someone.

Soda ash is not toxic, Tim tells us, but it can irritate nasal passages and cause some people to sneeze repeatedly. The men gathered at an "eatniche" for lunch seem at home in the underworld. Their powdery faces streaked with sweat, the miners joke with each other as they eat their sandwiches. Employees work what's called a 7-7-6 shift, switching between day and night shifts, and accumulating big chunks of time off. The unconventional schedule is one of the things they like about the job—they can take advantage of Wyoming's hunting and fishing. The average pay is $17.50 an hour with some good benefits, like triple pay on holidays. The average worker has been in the mine 13 years, and there are more than a few second-generation trona miners in Sweetwater County.

Going to work 1,500 feet underground is an unusual lifestyle. At the FMC mine near Green River, United Steelworkers Union shop steward Lee Ellis takes a break for lunch in an "eatniche." Miners can earn over $40,000 a year, working a rotating series of night and day shifts because the mine operates 24 hours a day.

Tim says trona mining takes constant attention to reduce the possibility of injury. After working for years in mines throughout the Southwest, he went back to school and got a degree in engineering. Now he's on the management side. The union shop steward kids him unmercifully for a while, asking, "So, you only good for giving tours now, Tim?"

"We've argued from opposite sides of the table more than once," says Tim. "Then we'll finish up—and play softball together on the FMC team," which is where they'll be this night, too.

Riding back up in the cage with two dozen miners, the first sight of daylight is a relief to the visitors. Looking across sagebrush and uncluttered landscape as we leave, it doesn't seem possible that underneath is that network of streets bigger than San Francisco's, populated by 425 people—the largest work force in the county. Above ground, there's little movement for miles, except for the cars arriving for the next shift and four antelope grazing in the afternoon sun.

As mining grows more technical, the number of scientific jobs connected with it increases. Many are in Laramie, where the University of Wyoming is located. Norman Merriam is an engineer studying ways to upgrade Wyoming coal for use in water purification and aluminum manufacturing. He works for the Western Research Institute of Laramie, a private, non-profit arm of the university. Its 150 scientists concentrate on energy and environmental problems.

Lorne Hickok remembers when the Amoco Refinery in Casper was the biggest employer in town. He stands at the tower with the bright lights of the refinery in the background. Despite the decline in oil prices, the Amoco Refinery is one of the surviving parts of a once dominant oil industry in Wyoming. Amoco Production Company was the state's largest oil producer in the 1980s, accounting for a fifth of the state's oil production.

Holly Skinner's new "job" is panning for gold in the Hoback Range near Pinedale. She has baked bread at the Miner's Delight restaurant, led wilderness expeditions, performed in a "Wild West" show, and written a book about her birthplace, called "Only the River Runs Easy." Some of her adventures are also good research for writing, she says.

CELEBRATING THE LAND

A prayer was said on the climb marking the fiftieth anniversary of

Glenn Exum's discovery of a major route up the Grand

Teton. The minister, a climber standing on a small rock

ledge above a two-thousand-foot drop to the valley floor,

said, "God, bless those who toil and play on your

mountain today."

For most of its recent history, Wyoming has attracted people who like the

combination of toil and play in challenging circumstances.

People who want the difficulties of climbing, camping or

kayaking in wild country come to enjoy the increasingly

rare, untouched land.

Grand Teton Park rangers John Carr and Bob Irvine are part of an elite group, trained to save the lives of climbers who are trapped or injured in the mountains. There are often several climbing deaths in the park in a summer. The rangers are assigned to a four day patrol at the saddle of the Grand Teton, elevation 11,000 feet.

LIVING IN WYOMING

Yellowstone National Park is dedicated to honoring the wild, but each summer it is home to a bizarre intermingling of humans and animals, with the species sometimes switching roles.

On a summer trip through the park, I found wild bighorn sheep who liked people, and a man who didn't. It wasn't easy to get to him, the fire watcher on Mount Washburn. He lived literally on top of a world that, far below him, teemed with people in search of a national park experience.

This journey began at the south entrance to the park. There, the idea that you're entering strange territory is reinforced by the message chalkboard. Just names are there. "John Train" is scrawled, as if John is a person so far gone into the wilds that the only way to reach him is to write his name on a board and hope he sees it. What happened? Did he leave postcards and a wallet at the hotel in Jackson, and a responsible clerk wants to send them back? Did his father die of a heart attack, so he'll return from days of fishing, a scraggly beard on his face, to find a parent not only dead, but mourned and buried, in his absence?

Those names on the board call to mind the reputed sign at the gate to hell. "Abandon Hope, All Who Enter Here" should be, "Abandon your cellular phone, Fed Ex doesn't reach here."

When so many acres of Yellowstone park burned in 1988, a wise ranger predicted the blackened trees wouldn't keep people away from the park. From the fifties, when you could feed your peanut butter sandwich to a bear, the animals and the steaming, bubbling thermal surprises have been the main attractions. As one young mother said, "I wondered if my kids would be bored. But a friend told me the place is just so weird that kids are fascinated." Her friend was right. Everywhere you go in the park, you find people stumbling toward large wild animals, sticking their fingers in boiling pools of water, and acting unsure as to whether this is a theme park or the real outdoors.

"They're ruint," said the reclusive fire watcher of the rare Big Horn sheep, who have taken to begging for food along a road through Yellowstone. The sheep graze among the purple fireweed, which thrives on the kind of ashy soil left by the massive Yellowstone fires of 1988.

On an August day at Lewis River, it was clear something was happening, from the clump of cars pulled over beside the road. The cars were stuck into the road shoulder and small parking lot like pickup sticks freshly scattered. The drivers were obviously in a hurry.

Just below the turnout, we saw why. A bull moose and a cow were grazing in the lush, almost chartreuse new meadow growth beside a tributary that flowed high, at the level of the reeds and grass. Thirty people, pointing 13 cameras, watched silently. Eleven had jumped out of a tour bus. The rest had come in eight other cars, from Indiana, Oregon, Minnesota, and elsewhere.

Below the turnout from the road, two men with cameras were trying to get close for pictures. One man slithered on his belly toward the bull moose. He moved forward five feet, the moose looked up ominously—and we held our breath.

Then came a Texas accent booming and crackling over a bullhorn.

"You are too close to the animals."

The crowd jumped at the noisy voice of authority.

"I will cite the man in the black tank top for getting too close to the animals."

People craned their necks to find the source of the bullhorn intrusion. A Park Service truck had joined the poorly parked cars.

"The meadow belongs to the moose."

He'd been building up to that line. It was intoned, rather than spoken. "Let's leave it to them," he added, a little more kindly. The man in the tank top was speaking German to his fellow travelers and seemed bewildered. People looked embarrassed for being caught staring at the moose, and the crowd broke up.

But spying on animals is part of the seductiveness of Yellowstone. A little further down the road at the West Thumb Ranger Station was a chalkboard like the one for messages at the park entrance. But this featured animal sitings.

"Elk near Grant Village, 5:20 pm" was scrawled there. And a map had little pins where animals had been seen. It's not animal ferocity, but human curiosity that leads to most encounters between species. More people are hurt trying to get close to bison every year than are attacked by bears.

"I will cite the man in the black tank top," boomed the Park Service voice of authority in Yellowstone National Park, warning tourists gathered to watch the moose munching grass in a meadow. Every year, some visitors are injured when they fail to realize the animals are wild, not props in a theme park.

Watching the animals is a major activity in Yellowstone. The elk herd has nearly 15,000, the bison number 2,300. Coyotes, moose, grizzly and black bears, and bald eagles are among the best known wildlife to be seen.

A fellow who ran a ski rental shop in southern California spent his vacation in the Cody hospital after a bison opened up his chest with a huge gash. His ski shop was called "Buffalo Bill's," and for obvious reasons he thought a picture of himself with a bison would look good in the shop. He made sure his ten-year-old son was safely in their van with the camera, then he walked up to the bison, intending to pose with his arm around its neck. The bison charged, hooked its horn into him, and tossed him toward his van. No picture, but 36 stitches.

Watching the rare bighorn sheep is safer, although normally they're very shy of humans. A good place to see them is on the trail up to the 10,317-foot summit of Mt. Washburn. On an August morning with a storm coming in, we took off up the foot path. The atmosphere at the beginning had been warm and comfortable, the hillside lush with small lavender, daisy-like flowers. In the distance was a color pattern that looked like half a rainbow: a stripe of light blue sky at the top, a glowing blue next, deep bluish-purple below that, then black tips of burned forest, and underneath it all, tender green shoots.

Like Jack on his beanstalk, we soon climbed through the clouds into a different world. It looked like the outdoors looks in March, with black trees against grey sky. This was one of the areas heavily burned in the 1988 fires. Some sunshine broke through once in a while, and for a moment the fireweed under the burned trees lit up in the sunlight. Fireweed flourishes in the ashy soil after a fire, and its bright pink color is gorgeous against the black trunks.

As the path reached 8,500 feet, a sign warned:

"No shortcuts.

Because of the short growing season

and severe conditions,

subalpine tundra may require a century

to recover from new trails."

It is quiet land, inhospitable to humans, but a favorite spot for the bighorn sheep, who can handle the rough terrain and minimal vegetation. Out of the burned, scrubby pines, three or four at a time, they came. We could hear them munching.

One looked up, a white flower hanging from its mouth. They were quiet and mysterious; they seemed like guerrilla fighters coming out of the protection of the trees. Finally there were twelve, moving across an extremely steep hill with sure steps, and some comical hops. A lamb lay down on the ground, just above the permanently frozen subsoil, then scrambled to catch the others. Hikers on the path were frozen, too, trying not to move and scare away the animals.

The path ended in a forbidding looking concrete structure on top of a pile of rocks for the fire watcher, one of three people in the park still living all fire season in a tower, scanning the 360-degree horizon for smoke in the vast wilderness. Other forests use airplanes to watch for fire, but in Yellowstone the romantic, old-fashioned method hangs on. The steep, cold, windy last half-mile of path inspires the hopeful hiker to expect a rustic and welcoming spot at the end of the journey. But climbing the last steps and pulling open the door led to a big surprise. There, in a room with windows on three sides, and a view like the one from an airplane . . . was a pay telephone.

And there was another stairwell, with a firm message taped to it:

"Do not disturb the fire watcher."

We came to see what life was like in the windowed room at ten thousand feet. Climbing up a metal ladder to the actual tower and knocking on the door did not go over well with the fire watcher, a wiry man who informed us he'd turned down "Good Morning, America" and "60 Minutes" and wasn't talking to anyone.

Park officials told us later that all three of the fire watchers are hermits. They take the job for the solitude, and even the most persistent hiker can't win an invitation to their retreats.

The fire watcher did leave us with a gruff complaint, after we told him about seeing the bighorn sheep.

"Damned sheep. I've been watchin' 'em all summer. They just go down to the road and beg for food. They've been ruint."

Yellowstone was the first national park. But this pioneer place, created for the purpose of preserving the wild, was far too tamed for the fire watcher.

Roy Renkin hugs a tree as part of his job as a biologist in Yellowstone. He's measuring the circumference of this one in an area where the effects of the 1988 fires are being studied. "There's a happy camper," he says of a new lodgepole pine sprout. His fascination with the forest floor is total. "I'd walk into a grizzly if he was standing in front of me because I'm always looking down," says Roy. Biologists view the fires as an overdue, necessary act of nature, and dozens of research projects are underway in Yellowstone to learn from them.

When huge fires swept through Yellowstone, they left a mosaic pattern of blackened areas next to untouched trees. Biologists say the park will provide better habitat for wildlife, creating an "explosion of songbirds" and more variety of open and sheltered spaces for grazing animals.

One summer in Jackson Hole, a college student, playing in a band for the summer season, did something amazing. He found what became the most popular route up the Grand Teton by making a leap of faith across a wide gap, with several thousand feet to fall if he failed.

Glenn Exum is now 78—unassuming and warm, with a soft voice that seems constantly on the verge of a chuckle. Over his shoulder out the window of his log home, you can see the Teton Range. He shakes his head when he talks about his achievement.

Exum's friend, Paul Petzoldt, was guiding two Austrians up the Grand on July 15, 1931, and Exum was along "for fun." At that time, people used the Owen-Spalding route up the 13,770-foot mountain, but Petzoldt thought an eastern ridge, one that looked like the jagged back of a dinosaur, might be promising. It led right to the top, in a direct line from the south.

Petzoldt said, "Hey, Ex, why don't you see if that ridge has a route up?" From below, the Grand Teton looks like a mountain cut out of cardboard and stuck against the sky. It seems like one straight line up the left side and down the right. But up close, that imposing grey wall is a pile of ridges full of places to put one foot, then another, and maybe enough steps to reach the top. Sixty years ago, Exum took off and came to the end of a ledge that's now called Wall Street. It's a place where you gasp at the sudden drop-off—1,500 feet of sheer space before the lower rocks, 6,000 feet to the valley floor. Glenn says he took one look, and turned back to the safety of the wide beginning of Wall Street. Petzoldt had said to shout if the route didn't work, and they'd come back for him. He shouted. The wind blew. And no one came. So Glenn ran back to the scary spot again. He did that seven times, but no one heard.

Then he made a decision. He climbed up a few feet above the ledge to get some momentum, leaped across—five impossible feet, held his ground, and began to climb.

After he turned 70, Glenn Exum finally quit climbing mountains, saying he "wouldn't want to disgrace any pile of rocks with a bad performance."

"I was afraid. No doubt about that," he says now. "But I was much more frightened when I looked back and saw what I'd done. I think I climbed that mountain through fear. The adrenaline was really cookin' in me, and I just took off like a jackrabbit and went up there. After that first foray, it looked kind of level."

This wasn't climbing where a guide at the top hollers, "Over to your left . . . a 'thank God' handhold," right when your muscles are worn out and shaking, while you try to figure out how not to fall backward into space. Exum made one move, then another, never knowing when the moves might lead to a dead-end cliff with no way up or down. No one had been there before, and he was climbing into the unknown. He did it alone, at the age of 20, in borrowed football shoes two sizes too large.

At a place called the Friction Pitch, there's nothing obvious to stand on, and his shoes slipped. But mostly the sections of climbing between safe ledges, called pitches, lived up to names climbers would later give them, names that catch the beauty of this sunlit ridge, such as Golden Stair. He reached the top, hours ahead of Petzoldt's party. Exum says when the two friends saw each other at the summit, Petzoldt ran across the rocks with the "two little Austrians," as he called them, tied to his climbing rope and bouncing along behind him.

The daring discovery went into the history books, and Exum went down the mountain, in a hurry to keep his date playing with a band in Jackson that night.

Petzoldt told Exum, "You're nuts, you know." But Exum says he got less crazy with age. He went to climb the Eiger in 1938, but "the rock was so lousy, we decided to go swimming."

At the climbing school founded by Glenn Exum and named for him, the modern world has crept in, but only a little.

"These ropes are heavy. No one uses them anymore, but the school must think they're safer," mutters first-year guide Jim Berwick, trying to make a neat coil. Modern ropes have fluorescent colors and lots of flexibility. These are grey and stiff. But Jim is himself the latest model climber, in hot-colored tights that live up to their name, two earrings in his left lobe, and an accent that the student climbers think might be French or Peruvian. The fact is, he's from Colorado. And he's standing beside Jenny Lake, instead of on a Peruvian mountainside, because of a very modern problem, the cost of insurance.

Jim spent ten years guiding wealthy forty and fifty-year-olds in the Andes. "They were looking for one last big adventure," says Jim, and they paid well for his help. He earned enough money to buy two houses. Now he realizes that one slip by a client, and he could have lost everything in a lawsuit. Even now, with an employer to worry about lawsuits and a safer elevation, he's still a nervous guy. Four of us sit on a ledge wide enough to stretch out our legs without dangling over the cliff. Fifteen-year-old Danny walks nonchalantly along the ledge to Jim for a rappeling lesson, and is told to go tie a rope around his waist before walking anywhere.

"It just takes seeing one body fall past to make you careful," says Jim, sobering up our cocky group.

Eight eyes ask silently, "Have you ever seen that?" Yes. Not one of his clients, though. The falling body was very quiet, we are told, though still alive when it passed Jim's spot on the rock. We shudder, and wonder what the person was thinking in the silent moment when Jim saw him on his way to death.

It happens. A staff of trained rescue rangers is on call all summer at Grand Teton National Park to save lives on the peaks or, as ranger John Carr puts it, "to carry out the body bags."

"Dying is part of living," smiles Jim, in a hopeless attempt to make our eyes less wide and our nerves more calm.

Mountain guide Jim Berwick watches a would-be rock climber's most important asset—his feet. An instructor for the Exum Mountain Guides in the Tetons, he tells students to take as many steps up a small practice rock as their age, urging them to imitate a dancer's moves on the rocks.

The class has learned how to tie knots, throw ourselves off 100-foot cliffs and rappel down under our own control, and move cat-like over the rocks as demonstrated by our guides. Now we have hiked up a mile in elevation to the moonscape saddle below the Grand Teton at over 11,000 feet. On this day, a cold, wet climb ended with a wait in the rain for a chance to struggle up the last rock cliff to the saddle through a stream running down the way we were climbing up.

There's a hut kept by the climbing school on the saddle, and the wet cold outside makes the shelter especially sweet. It's one of the major feelings of climbing—a grueling experience that heightens the beauty of the moment when the pain stops. During the night we were startled by roars and cracks of thunder, coming together with brilliant flashes of lightning. Electrical storms near the top of a mountain have stunning impact. We shook with the storm as if we'd stumbled into its territory and were being warned. Again, it was the delicious juxtaposition of threat and safety. Our skin seemed such a fragile outer layer before what the skies had to offer.

The day did not dawn with bird song and sunshine. It came in dissension and disappointment. The guides said ice and hail would coat the ledges we were planning to climb. But a former Army skier named Chip, wearing camouflage rain gear, was adamant. He stood on a rock with his chin stuck out, and said he was going. It wasn't clear whether he planned to wait for a guide.

We finally all left for the summit three hours later when the sky cleared. And our fear of a new sudden storm added a chill to a deadly area we crossed. It was the gully before the Wall Street that Glenn Exum had followed to his famous new route. In that place, one climber had been found in 1986, caught in his frozen rope. He lived. But three others froze as they desperately followed the wrong gully, after a night of trying to get off the mountain, fatally slowed by hypothermia and confusion. They had gotten to the summit, wearing summer clothes, and been caught in 80-mile-per-hour winds and snow on the way down. One mistake followed another, and they left their mark on the mood of the mountain. The opposite happened to us on our climb.

Passing time while on patrol in the mountains, ranger John Carr is prepared for the hours of waiting and watching. He brings a portable chess set. Climbing guide Ken Jern joins him in a game, while ranger Bob Irvine watches from the door of a hut maintained by the Park Service.

As we went higher, it grew warmer. Stepping carefully where Glenn Exum had leaped, my fingers were stiff with cold, bare because gloves would get in the way of climbing. Reaching for a hold on the rock felt like grasping ice cubes and holding on for dear life. But the sun began to thaw the ice on the rocks. In the afternoon, we reached black rock that retained the sun's heat. You become very aware of your hands, when they connect you to the rock and to safety. As the rock warmed, it felt as welcome and reassuring as a loaf of just-baked bread.

Reaching the summit was not the peak of the experience. For me, it was the moments of grace on paths crossed by so many people, balanced against the fear of looking past a foot to valleys a mile below. It was the contrasts: the struggle and the resolution, the fierce focus and ecstatic release.

For Glenn Exum, the reward of 300 trips to the top of the Grand in 50 years was "the people. I told them, 'The more you suffer down here, the less you suffer up there,' when I was teaching them. And I always showed them the little flowers and the kinds of rock. I had a great privilege, seeing the mountains, and showing them to people."

Most attempts to climb to the summit of the Grand begin at the hut on the saddle, then follow along the right skyline ridge of the mountain to the peak, the second highest point in Wyoming.

"We'll be off the summit by 10:00 a.m.," the guide tells a group of teenaged climbers, as they gaze to the top of the 13,770-foot Grand Teton from the saddle 2,500 feet below. They'll spend the night in a hut on the saddle, then get started before daybreak to be up and down from the peak before afternoon storms come in, sometimes bringing deadly lightning, hail and surprise snows.

Wyoming is a good place to learn about surviving in a cold climate. The Lander-
based National Outdoor Leadership School, NOLS, is one of several organizations
offering winter expeditions. On this trip, three instructors teach 16 people, ranging
in age from 18 to 26, how to live without much support from the modern world.
They do without tents and freeze-dried food. Their dedication to leaving no litter
is so strong they don't even use toilet paper—snowballs are mandatory, even at 30
degrees below zero. That's not the worst of it, according to one teenager—during
the desert camping trip they had to use sticks.

The students range in experience from a professional, "sponsored" snowboarder to a young woman who had never camped before. By the end of the 90 days, their talk is almost exclusively of the hot showers, rich food, and good parties they are craving. Most think outdoor training is worth the physical and monetary cost.

CONTINUITY

*O*ne appeal of living in Wyoming is the power of its past. Some people are haunted with the lives that were lived before because of the danger, excitement, and romantic freedom of those lives. To celebrate the state's centennial in 1990, several hundred people rode covered wagons along the historic Jim Bridger Trail, calling home on cellular phones, but feeling firsthand the closeness and irritation born of the troubles of rough travel. Indians on the Wind River Reservation struggle to gain strength from their spiritual heritage. And a few people, such as Snook and Evalyn Moore, still live richly without the modern world, enjoying a Wyoming that for most people survives only in dreams of the past.

A hundred years ago they were enemies. But now the Arapaho and Shoshone tribes share two million acres in central Wyoming—the Wind River Reservation. The two tribes retain their separate identities, and some animosities. But they work together to keep alive traditions, such as the summer powwow, a weekend of competitive dance and music.

*Arapaho elders Earl La Bean, Leo Jenkins, Robert Sun Roads, and Melvin Hatt
watch the dancing at a special powwow on Father's Day, held to honour elders.
Among duties of the elders are keeping the ceremonial drum and teaching children
about tribal traditions.*

At some powwows, children are given a prize just for dressing up and dancing.
Many of their costumes took weeks to create.

Vincent Redman is an elder in the Arapaho Tribe on the Wind River Indian Reservation. He wears a cowboy hat over his short hair, smokes menthol cigarettes, and teaches children about sacred traditions.

"Two of my grandsons have hair that's never been cut," he says proudly, calling nine-year-old Sonny over. Sonny stops tossing a basketball at the hoop mounted between two logs and comes over, smiling at us. His three black braids hang to his waist.

Inside Vincent's house, another grandson looks out at us. His hair is cut almost punk style, and his T-shirt reads, "Lifestyles of the poor and unknown."

On the clothesline a quilt blows in the wind, hand-stitched in a star pattern of red, blue, and purple. It's the work of Vincent's youngest daughter, who studies old reservation patterns and recreates them. One of the sons is getting a degree in forestry at the University of Wyoming. Vincent is proud of him, too.

Mixing the old and the new is the current style on the reservation, which already combines two tribes so different that their forced togetherness in Wyoming is like assigning Arabs and Israelis to the same lifeboat. The Shoshone and Arapaho tribes came to the Wind River Indian Reservation as enemies, stuck together on two million acres by the U.S. government. But they share a new effort to give back to the children some of the cultural inheritance lost in a century of evolving reservation life.

Decades of discouragement on the reservation came to a head in 1985, when nine young men from the tribes committed suicide over a two-month period. The talk at the time was of an ailing society, infected by unemployment, alcohol abuse, and pointlessness. Before economic development efforts got started to deal with those problems, tribal leaders reached back into their spiritual heritage for answers. A sacred pipe ceremony was held. The suicides stopped.

"I got a boy going to college to study forestry, and two grandsons who have never cut their hair," says Vincent Redman, an elder in the Arapaho Tribe. His grandson, Sonny, has the traditional braids Vincent was not permitted to grow when he went to St. Michael's boarding school. He wasn't allowed to "speak Indian" either, but now he teaches youngsters the old language as part of a new effort to restore traditions and mend some of the destructive habits plaguing the Wind River Indian Reservation.

Now there are language camps in summer and culture classes in winter, all taught by elders, four of whom are women. Vincent Redman has been an elder since he was 50—he's now 61. His smile seems about right for his age, but his body seems to have gone through a lot more. Arthritis has gnarled his hands, and one shows a scar where an effort was made to fix things. His hips are very stiff, and his walk shows pain, as he leads us to the porch of his new red house, given to him because he's considered disabled.

"Mind if I get me a smoke?" he asks. He performs what seems like the impossible task of lighting a cigarette with bent hands, and says, "I teach games, how to tan hides and how to survive by fishing, slashing meat, how to dry it, how to cut and wash the hide." And as often as once a week, he takes the youngsters into a traditional sweat lodge "to purify themselves." Rocks are heated and all ages and sexes breathe the steam and experience this old tradition.

Vincent also teaches the Arapaho language—the one he was not allowed to use when he was uprooted to St. Michael's boarding school on the reservation at age six. "When I first started to know things," he says, "I talked Indian. They changed me when I went to school. If you talked Arapaho, you got in trouble." Every week, from Sunday night through Friday he lived in the mission where the language he spoke on weekends wasn't permitted. And he knew not to wear the traditional braids—he'd heard the stories of his father's long hair being forbidden in earlier days of reservation school. Do the kids sometimes think learning a language other than English is stupid? "Yeah, they do sometimes. But sometimes not."

"We are going along with the modern world, and keeping the old," says another Arapaho, Byron Yellowbear. He was describing how his family of six is teaching the youngest, a two-year-old girl, to speak. The family sits around after dinner and "she repeats everything we say." She's learning mostly English, and a few Arapaho words. Byron also takes the children to a weekly powwow in the summer, where all the children are given five dollars just for dancing in costumes.

William and Wind Thunder Tarness wait while their father John shops at an agriculture project run by Arapaho Indians. The project was started to help solve the high unemployment rate on the reservation. There were 136 applications for eight jobs on the farm south of Ethete.

Byron is participating in both the spiritual and political movements on the reservation. He works for a new business owned by Indians. Today he stands under the snow-covered Wind River Mountains, and tugs a pipe into position in a drainage ditch . . . sending a stream of water down a row of barley. It's irrigating time, one of June's first warm days. He smiles broadly. "They had 136 applications for this job, and hired eight of us."

Unemployment on the reservation is estimated as high as 70 percent, so Byron's pride at having a job makes sense. And there's more. "I'm learning something," he says. After a year of buying equipment and getting started, the project is expected to make money this summer. "We're looking at a quarter of a million dollars on our barley crop alone," says Byron. "We're hoping to get a bonus." Then they plan to buy cattle to feed through the winter, selling for profit in the spring.

Byron is only a laborer in this job, but he's thinking about his future. "My own place, that's what I want," he says. "Say in three years, I'm hoping to get a little herd going. You get you five to eight yearlings, raise 'em, and build up a herd. I got brothers and sisters I been trying to talk into buying a place like this," he says, pointing to the satisfying little piece of land he's working. It's green, gently rolling irrigated earth—the heart's desire of a would-be farmer-rancher. A year ago, the field was covered with six feet of weeds.

Down the hill there's another change. Spring runoff water has been stored in a small lake that was little more than a puddle before. Now it's habitat for fish and birds. "People been pulling nine-inch brown trout out of it," says Byron.

Indians got a boost from a U.S. Supreme Court ruling upholding an earlier court decision that the tribes have first rights to 500,000 acre-feet of water flowing through the reservation. The new Arapaho farm project uses some of the water. And the tribes want to keep enough in the Wind River to prevent it from drying out on occasion. With a steady supply of water, they can stock trout and develop fishing.

Face paint is a dramatic part of Wayne Perdash's costume for a powwow at Arapahoe. Indian dancers can travel to a different event each weekend in Wyoming and surrounding states on a kind of powwow circuit. Many of their costumes are traditional, but others are new, to express the wearer's creativity.

But the Supreme Court decision wasn't the last word. Giving water to the tribes takes it away from some old-time users. There's only so much water in a state with an average rainfall of 12 to 16 inches a year. The court decision means the Indians get first choice, since their rights are older than those of ranchers who bought reservation lands. Keeping the river at a level high enough for the trout could mean denying water to some farmers for their crops. Wyoming politicians came to the aid of those ranchers, attempting to keep the Indians from using all their water at the expense of the ranchers.

Crops and cattle are economic forces in Fremont County, where most of the reservation is located. And farmers have bitterly questioned whether enough tourists would come for the fishing to make it worth the downfall of longtime farms.

Reaching ahead to a better economy has landed the Indians back in one of the oldest struggles in the West—the one over water. How to use Wyoming's resources is the new battleground, vividly expressed in the struggle between people who want water for crops and those who hope to develop fishing and a tourism industry. Deny the farmers with lesser water rights, and some will lose money, maybe their farms as well. Deny the development efforts, and pay the price in dashed hopes for a society trying to rebuild itself. Even the U.S. Supreme Court wasn't able to put this one to rest.

The powwow is a social occasion that lasts for a weekend. Dancing starts in the morning, may go on past midnight, with everyone from the elderly to babies staying up late.

In Wyoming's Centennial year, 1990, people marked the occasion by riding horses and covered wagons along the historic Jim Bridger Trail from Casper to Cody. The idea of crossing the plains and mountains to a new life "out West" appeals powerfully to our imaginations, especially in a state still marked by wheel ruts and roadside graves from the wagon train riders of 140 years ago. At times, up to two thousand people joined in the Centennial trip to Cody.

One-year-old Star Whitt came along for the full thirty days, accompanied by her family of five and seasoned riders such as Tom Angle. One hundred and forty-two people traveled for the entire month, but at times as many as two thousand were on the trail.

For Anne McCune, keeping the horses watered was a constant necessity.
Rattlesnakes were caught on the trail and eaten, rowdy cowboys were expelled,
and the riders grew as nostalgic as they hoped they would. The trip helped them
relive some of the heat, dust, discomfort, and close friendships natural to a
caravan of strangers sharing a purpose as well as physical hardship.

Jim Silber runs a day care center with his wife, Julie, when he's not re-enacting the life of a mountain man. Artist James Bama, who traveled with the wagon train, says, "My fantasy is painting people living out their fantasy."

We'd met three people in the Green River Valley, and each one said, "Have you met Snook Moore?" He's been here forever, they told us, and "his wife, Evalyn—what a beauty."

The directions were a bit hazy. "Drive down to the end of that field, and follow the road by the barn, the little barn. He's probably out haying right now," said Joe. We bumped along up the side of the hill and changed our minds, turning back down the hill, then around another barn and through some willows. We thought we were lost, and maybe this Snook didn't want to meet us anyway. Before we could lose our nerve, three cabins appeared. They weren't exactly abandoned, but their posture wasn't great, either. And a dirt road beckoned across a stream through more willows. Beyond, smoke rose from a long, low cabin.

The man standing in front was shockingly bent over, but his face told a different story. It was open and smiling, as if he'd known we were coming for months and we'd been sent by his dearest friend.

Snook had been in great demand in the forties because he was so good at breaking horses. Once a rancher stopped him on the street in Reno to try to steal him away from another. "Cowboy, you want a job?" the rancher said. "Ninety dollars and all the beans you can eat. And the heaviest thing you pick up is your saddle."

But Snook dreamed of having his own place on the Green River, and the horses had done their share of breaking *him*. His hips, his ribs, his legs all gave way under hard falls from wild horses. He has the hunched posture to remind him.

An odd couple, Snook and his wife Evalyn met at a dance when she was the new schoolmarm from California, and he was a shy cowboy in a "valley full of 40 bachelors." A neighbor recently insisted on running a water pipe to their cabin. But they live now as they did in the thirties—without electricity, telephone or mail delivery. The one time Evalyn took Snook shopping "in town" (Pinedale, pop. 1,061), he got spooked by "all the noise" and had to go home.

But Snook's look is not defeated. He is treasured by friends collected in a long lifetime, and he shows it. One small evidence of this was tied around his neck— a bright blue, pure silk cowboy scarf, sent to him by a female artist who makes them in Jackson Hole. It matched his eyes exactly.

He led us into the cabin as though it were planned all along. The cabin was a creation that just grew, arranged like a series of railroad cars. We walked through the mud room where boots were piled, through the kitchen, smelling of long-simmering stew and a wood-stove fire, down a hall with a narrow bed in it, into a room with lushly weathered, glowing reddish-brown wood walls.

The wood showed in small patches, but mostly the walls were covered with photographs, sketches, and framed notes. "I love you, Grandpa Snook," read one.

Evalyn sat at the rough wood table, which was as covered as the walls. It held heaps of magazines, books and letters. She did have the beautiful skin her neighbors described. And she did not look the nearly 90 years they thought she must have lived. Evalyn had two pre-teen daughters and years of teaching experience when she came to the Green River Valley in 1933. She left Palo Alto, California, after the stock market crash and the beginning of the Depression because "it was too hard to get teaching jobs." She began what she called "vagabond teaching, taking schools that were interesting" in Utah and Wyoming. And then she was assigned to Green River.

"All that valley was sawmills, ranches, and old bachelors," she said. "There were 40 bachelors." She met Snook at a Christmas dance, which he says was kind of an unusual place for him to be. He was normally guiding pack trips or tending animals at a nearby dude ranch.

Snook was the third baby in Pinedale, with homesteading parents and a gold-miner granddad who trapped in Yellowstone. His uncle paid the taxes on the 160-acre ranch that was abandoned by its original homesteader. Then Snook and Evalyn took over the struggle to make the ranch work.

"After we bought this place, we had to build her up. Eighteen, 19-hour days," said Snook.

Evalyn added, "We didn't have money to buy wheat for the chickens. One of our hunters didn't have money enough to pay for the hunting trip. So we traded the hunting trip for wheat. And we did that for quite a few years."

Snook: "He came every year on his birthday, for 25 years."

Evalyn: "In the winter, we were just as busy. People always say, what in the world do you do? We worked, buildin' in the winter. And he fed the elk (working for the state). For 19 years."

Snook: "Twelve miles over that-a-way, and I snowshoed that damn trail from the first of January to the first of April, every day. Beside feeding the elk, I worked here at the ranch."

Evalyn: "I guess it did take a while gettin' started. We never had to advertise. The second year, our hunters got 46 elk."

Snook: "They'd ask the game and fish checker where to hunt. They'd say all the elk's coming out of Moore's place. I'd hunt all day and pack at night. The hunters'd sleep, and I'd have to go back for the elk, so I'd be ready to go huntin' in the morning."

Evalyn: "And then we had only three gentle horses, the rest were all outlaw horses. Some were given to us to get rid of."

Snook: "And I broke all those horses, sure. Tough work and a hard life," he said of those days.

Evalyn: "We worked."

Snook: "God, I should say."

Snook takes about twice as long to say a sentence as anyone I know. It wouldn't surprise me if I heard Henry Fonda had learned how to talk in westerns from Snook. They share a soft drawled emphasis, that lets each word roll off the tongue and grab your attention.

In the second winter, the elk feeding got a little easier. Instead of going on snowshoe the 24 miles each day, Snook got a dog team of collies and shepherds. And the couple began a lifelong passion for the dogs that shared their work.

Snook: "The first year for the dog team a big dog come in here."

Evalyn: "Beautiful."

Snook: "Poor damn dog, we never knew where he come from."

Evalyn: "We called him Teddy. He was three-fourths border collie and one-fourth coyote."

Snook: "Smartest dog I ever saw. Unbelievable. Taught him to wrangle milk cows. I'd tell him, 'Teddy, go get the milk cows.' He'd go look for them. He never missed.

He got 'em all."

I asked how he knew when he had them all, since he couldn't count, we could assume.

Snook: "He knew. He'd go look right in the willows and everything for 'em."

Evalyn: "And we had a colt that went with us after the cows, he decided to bring the cows in."

Snook: "By God, he did."

Evalyn: "He got rough."

Snook: "Two years old, and ever' night when I went out to wrangle the cows he'd come right with me. He knew the right time."

Evalyn: "They know the time."

Snook: "He'd bring 'em in. If they didn't run, he'd *bite* 'em. It was hard on the milk cows. I finally had to tie him up."

Evalyn: "When it was milkin' time. That horse was disappointed, because he thought he was helpin'. They all thought they were helpin'."

There was a dog, Pete, who became crippled, blind and deaf. But when Snook hooked up the dog team, he would stand in his spot in the traces. They tried locking him in the cabin, but he howled the entire time the dog team was gone. "He just cried," said Evalyn.

Snook: "I finally got him so he'd foller behind the dogsled, then when he'd play out, I'd put him on the sled with me."

The dog sled was about as much mechanized help as Snook would accept. As he will tell you, he doesn't like machinery. He grows and harvests hay without a tractor or any modern equipment. Horses pull his buck rake. His working truck is a '54 Chevy. But human help is another matter. The Moores have taken in a variety of young helpers over the years.

After a few years of Evalyn doing all the cooking and Snook the outfitting, they brought in a boy from the Church World Service to give him a job.

Evalyn said, "He grew up here, he helped us. And we had boys from orphanages in Denver. And then it just seemed like there were children popping in. I don't know how many there's been."

Snook said, "You live in this quiet, quiet country up here. Then you go into one of those cities, and the noise nearly drives you crazy. And it's all the time. It never quits."

Snook described how they popped in. "A couple arrived from California. The jeep pulled up the yard and the sheriff said, 'I got your boys here.' I said I don't know what you mean, I ain't got no boys. He said, 'Well here they are,' and I didn't know a thing in the world about it."

Evalyn: "Well, I met their mother on a trip to California, and she was going to give them away, so I took 'em, but I told her not to send 'em until I got back to the ranch. But she was afraid I'd change my mind. They missed the bus from Rock Springs to Pinedale and were standing there. The Highway Patrol stopped. They said they were going to Snook Moore's ranch, so the patrolmen stopped the bus. Of course, it was a surprise to Snook."

Snook: "They were good boys."

Evalyn: "They turned out well. They all did."

Snook had many jobs while building up the outfitting business. In the first year, he "ran a trap line. Anything for money." In the forties he hired out, breaking horses in California and Nevada. He also worked for the state game and fish department, stocking fish in high-country lakes.

"Boy I'm tellin' you, those Wind Rivers. There's a thousand lakes in those mountains. I stocked a hell of alot of 'em, packed 'em in on horses. They use round cans. You just hang straps and buckle them to the packsaddle horse."

But he also carried in fish on foot.

"Now there's one lake up there, Bear Lake, and I had to pack 'em in on my back three miles. I took 25 thousand fish pretty close on horses, then took 'em the rest of the way on my back. I went up after two years to see how they were doin'. I fished the inlet, and caught one—five pounds."

Evalyn: "They were fed with shrimp."

Snook: "You could look in there when the sun was shinin' and the wind wasn't blowin', and the water was all pink."

Evalyn: "Finest eatin' there is."

Snook: "Now, they use the helicopters. They stock the lakes with those."

The Moore ranch had been homesteaded in 1918 by a young veteran of World War I. According to Snook, "He stayed on it til he proved up on it. He left for . . ."

Evalyn: "We never knew where."

During the winter, Snook lives alone on the ranch, while Evalyn visits her daughter in San Diego. The ice and snow are too tough for her to navigate with a walker.

Snook: "Chicago or somewhere."

He lowered his voice to storytelling range.

"I'll never forget it. I was workin' out in the yard when a Cadillac drove up."

Evalyn: "With a chauffeur in livery."

Snook: "Over across the bridge is the orginal homesteaded cabin. He got out of the car, went over to the cabin, and patted it."

Evalyn: "Tears were drippin' down his face."

Snook: "Yeah, and I come walkin' out. I didn't know who he was. And so . . . "

Evalyn: "He said, 'I was happier here than I've ever been.'"

Snook: "'Than I ever was in my whole life.' And I said, 'Did you homestead this place?' And he said 'Yes I did. I'm Westman.' I said to him, I said, 'Why did you let it go if you felt that way about it?' He said, 'When I lost this place, I didn't have an extry shirt on my back.'"

Evalyn: "He couldn't make it."

Snook: "He went to Chicago, and he was makin' furniture, and he made a fortune. He had a chauffeur and he had a young wife with him."

Evalyn: "Beautiful young wife."

Snook: "Yup."

Evalyn: "And he wanted to stay here."

Snook: "He wanted to stay all night. He wanted to know if he could. And I said, 'Sure, if you want to.'"

Evalyn: "We just had the one cabin. And we told him we'd be glad to have him stay. But his wife said no, she'd made reservations."

Snook: "At the Wort Hotel."

Evalyn: "In Jackson. But the chauffeur told us that he had a heart condition and she wanted him to be near a doctor."

Snook: "Too bad."

Evalyn: "And he only lived a little while after he was here. But he just begged to stay."

Snook: "But I think he'd a been happier if he'd just died here."

Evalyn: "He'd been happier, because he patted that old cabin and said, 'Please promise me you'll never tear it down as long as you have this place.' So we promised him, and we never would. That's where we lived when we first got married."

They built a large lodge next door to the cabin, big enough for two pianos and seven mounted deer heads. "I sure had some trophies," said Snook. The lodge burned one winter several years ago, while Evalyn was in California and only Snook was there.

"I cried," said Evalyn. Along with the pianos, she lost a manuscript she'd written about the animals they've known. In addition to the working dogs and horses, there was an elk raised on a bottle when he was found an orphan. A horse named "Peanuts" took care of him, according to Evalyn.

Her fondness for the animals extended to the chickens. "One old hen who had a goatee, I don't know how old she was. But she walked just like me. She was crippled. One day I was out at the chicken house and I was talkin' to her, and she was talkin' to me, and she got up in the nest and went through all the motions of layin' an egg. And I knew she was too old to lay an egg. But she went through all these motions and she laid the biggest egg that I have ever seen from a hen.

"The next morning she was dead. That was her last gift. Poor old thing."

For twelve years now, Evalyn has spent winters in San Diego with her daughter. She uses a walker to get around, and in the snow, she's bedridden. Snook knew the date she left last year, November 5th. It's always "when the snow flies." Soon after that, deep snow closes the road to the ranch, and Snook is settled in for the winter to care for the animals. Wood is piled up and his food is stored in a root cellar.

"It's better than a refrigerator," he says. It has ventilation. "No mold, like those electric ones."

In spring, Evalyn waits until the road clears and she can return.

"I grew up in this country," says Snook.

"So you wouldn't go to California?" I asked.

"No, he'd be miserable," answered Evalyn.

He laughed. "That's true. You live in this quiet, quiet country up here. Then you go into one of those cities, and the noise nearly drives you crazy. And it's all the time. It never quits."

"Can you imagine Pinedale (population 1,061) being too busy for anybody?" asked Evalyn. "He came with me shopping about three years ago. There was a bunch of motorcycles, we couldn't find a parkin' place, there was music comin' out of one of the bars, and we just got things started, and Snook says, 'I gotta get outta here.' I said, 'Snook, we're not half through.' And he said, 'I gotta get outta here.' So I had to bring him home, he couldn't take it. I said, 'I'll never take you to town again.' And he said, 'That just suits me fine.'"

They laughed together for a while.

When you're not with Snook and Evalyn, you feel doubly sorrowful in advance, thinking about their age and eventual passing from the Green River. They embody a life of wood fires, treasured animals, adventures in a wild country, good long friendships. So many of us long for what they lived. Because they saw it, we see it too. And they are one of the great couples, gently laughing at each other, finishing each other's sentences, and sadly living apart five cold months of the year rather than make her uncomfortable or him claustrophobic. But when you're with Snook and Evalyn, there's no advance nostalgia, because they aren't of a sentimental past. They are thinking about getting the hay in to feed the animals through the winter and keeping the fire going. They have humor, hard work, and well-aged affection, which persist past the time of fish-teeming lakes and dogsled trips across a fresh unspoiled land.

"I'm a thinkin' I'm gonna get company," says Snook Moore, gazing across his fields at a puff of dust in the distance. Behind him are the truck he uses for work and the original homestead cabin on his ranch in the Upper Green River area. After "breaking nearly every bone" in his body as a cowboy, Snook bought his own piece of land in 1935, and settled down to guiding hunting and fishing trips.

At an old campground near the Teton-area town of Kelly is a yurt village. Yurts are Mongolian structures built of wood and canvas, originally designed to be packed up quickly by nomad tribes. A central bathhouse provides toilets, showers, and a place to do dishes. A teepee is used for meditation.

The structures have room for socializing. By building different levels, residents can isolate areas used for cooking, sleeping or working. Several have phones and computers. The yurt dwellers like their round space, the price (about $5,000) and the communal lifestyle.

COMMUNITY

I once heard a joke about why people in Wyoming are so friendly. "After driving a hundred miles and seeing nothing but a jackrabbit," the punch line goes, "I realized it was because they're lonely."

People go to great lengths to see each other, whether they're celebrating the arrival of summer, playing polo, or attending a sheepherders' fair, a dance, even an exercise class.

We found old folks who drive half a day to swim and stretch together in the warm pools of Thermopolis. Isolated ranchers who don't even have children attend the annual spring concert in a "nearby" one-room school house—15 miles down a dirt road.

When they do connect, the mood is usually competitive, joking, or gossipy. Just the usual ingredients of good friendship.

Towns invent their own traditions, even in the 1990s, and Casper Mountain's Crimson Dawn Celebration is one such home-grown gathering. Mountain resident Neal Forsling began celebrating the summer solstice Druid-style with her children. Soon the event grew, as friends dressed like characters in stories invented by Forsling. The "Lavender Witch" stands in front of Forsling's grave, on the land she donated for a county park at her death.

A bonfire is built at the end of the evening, when throwing a handful of dirt into the flames is supposed to bring good luck. The Druid trappings of the party have drawn picketers, who try to convince the party-goers the event is blasphemous.

At this mountain elevation of 8,000 feet, the arrival of summer is a major event, ending eight months of snow. Hundreds of people come to meet the costumed characters and enjoy the sunset on the longest day of the year.

*A traditional square dance skirt looks best with 160 yards of petticoat under it. At
the Maverick Square Dance Club in Casper, men are required to wear dress shirts
and women colorful dancing skirts. Twenty couples meet two Saturdays a month
at the old Officers Club on the abandoned air base. They maintain the building,
with its "great dance floor" and painted murals created in the 1940s. "We do it for
fellowship and exercise," says Darlene Eddy.*

"*I always wanted to be in the Dandies, as long as I can remember,*" *said one young woman from Cheyenne. Sixteen girls between 14 and high school graduation age are chosen to perform in horse routines at Cheyenne Frontier Days. They audition with their horses, and their riding ability is more important than their good looks. "We can make them pretty if they can ride," says Dandies manager, Arlene Kensinger.*

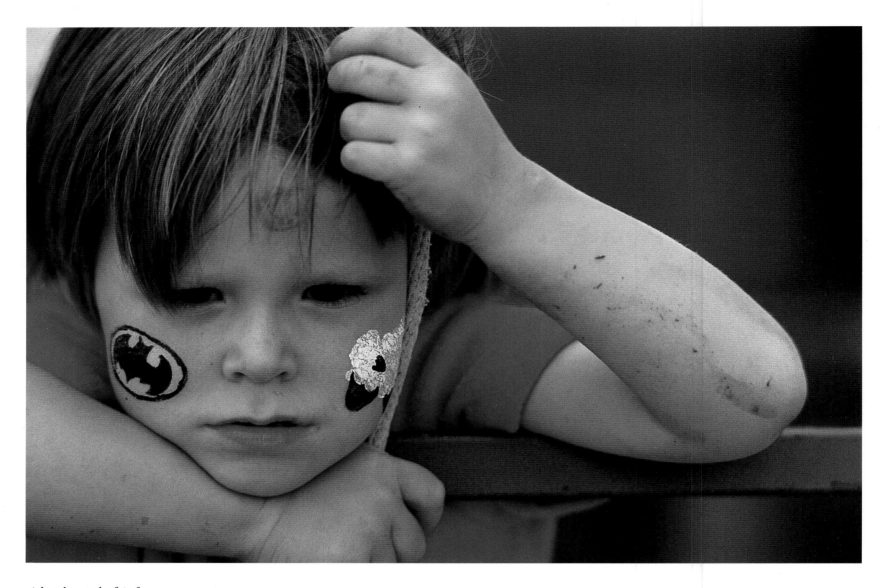

A hot day at the fair for a young spectator

The warm waters from the huge natural hot spring in Thermopolis are pumped into various public pools in the town. At the Star Plunge, exercise classes are offered in the water for people with arthritis, and they attract participants from 100 miles away. Cliff Coverson is recovering from surgery, trying to build up strength and flexibility in the pool.

The teacher is also the janitor at a one-room school house, so Robert Phinney
makes sure the muddy boots are left outside. He was on a waiting list for a
country school before getting this assignment. One kindergartner has been known
to show up on days he's not due at school so he won't miss anything.

In 35 Wyoming schools, life is like it was a hundred years ago in one important way: there is one teacher for the entire student body. Cathy Gardner's Billy Creek School looks like a small wing of a typical school, except that her apartment is at the end of the hall. The hall smells like a primary school. It looks like one, with its rows of boots, and hooks hung with sweaters and raincoats. But when you open the door at one end, you are in Miss Gardner's living room. The situation blurs the lines between teacher and student. One morning Cathy overslept. When she woke up late, she threw on a bathrobe and slippers, then went outside to bring in bottled water. That was the moment the school bus arrived, giving the children a good close look at their teacher in her nightclothes.

Cathy has taught for nine years in a one-room school that mostly serves ranch children near Crazy Woman Canyon, 20 miles from the town of Buffalo. She points out that the teaching ratio of one to 11 can't be beat (except in even smaller one-room schools). And she says that teaching the same children for five years, from kindergarten through fourth grade, lets her know the children so well that the usual months of review at the beginning of the year are cut in half. This protected way of life has its drawbacks. When the 10-year-olds plunge into a bigger school "in town," they go through a period of adjustment, dealing with children they haven't known all their lives.

In the course of a day, Robert Phinney, who teaches at the Kearney School, will notch a stick with the kindergartner to mark how many school days have passed. The stick came from a story he read the class about an Indian boy. The fourth-grader in the class will read the book and write an essay about it, while the youngest practices numbers by counting the stick's notches. It takes creativity to use one book to teach a five-year-old and a ten-year-old at the same time. And as Robert says, it also takes a family-style helping out among the students. He and Cathy agree that one strength of the one-room school is the way older students help teach the younger ones. They say their students do better than average when they move on.

The old school house just below Fort Phil Kearney was painted red in time for the state's centennial. It's one of three dozen one-room school houses in Wyoming.

Aside from the educational advantages, these two young teachers prefer the way of life at a country school. Cathy says she likes the solitude, but that any of the parents would drop whatever they were doing to help her. Robert was on a waiting list for a school like the one he has now, with its impossibly scenic spot under the snowy mountains. He rides his horse to school occasionally. On a less romantic note, he and Cathy, like all teachers in one-room schools, also handle the janitorial duties.

Even farther down a country road is the Hanging Woman School in Sheridan County. One of the stories about how it got its name involves a woman so lonely in the northern Wyoming hills that she hanged herself. This idea strikes Paula Brown as ridiculous. Paula teaches five children at the school, lives in a trailer five feet from the dusty playground, and loves her life.

She doesn't even clear out of her remote spot in the summer. Instead, she sets up a volleyball net for nearby ranch hands and anyone else looking for some company. The sense of family is everywhere at her school. Each student's name is carefully carved on a wooden sign reading, "Hanging Woman School—Paula Brown, Teacher."

She is made of the stuff required for modern one-room school teachers. She calmly stored a rabid bat in her freezer until it could be taken to a lab for tests, she drives 18 miles to pick up mail that only comes three times a week, and she makes her tiny school house a social center for nearby ranch families.

Outside her home is a satellite dish. Paula tapes shows and movies for her neighbors, and loans them the tapes when they come to pick up their kids. Her students' spring concert brought a full house to the 12-by-15-foot room. It was one of the rare bits of genuine entertainment in the northern reaches of Sheridan County.

For nine years, teacher Cathy Gardner has lived at the end of the hall at the Billy Creek School. She likes the solitude in her little apartment, which is fortunate, since she's 20 miles from the town of Buffalo. Once she's had students for five years, they attend a candlelight dinner to celebrate graduating from fourth grade and moving on to a school in town. "Usually everyone's in tears," says Cathy.

Ryan Bulkley removes his hat on the way in to the Hanging Woman School after recess. When Ryan pays a weekly visit from the Fence Creek School, where he's the only student, teacher Paula Brown lets the kids have extra time to play. "They need some time to socialize," she says.

Paula Brown teaches a brother and sister in her Hanging Woman School student body of five. The youngest is five-year old Lacey Benton. While Paula reads to Lacey, the 11-year old does math, the 10-year old works on a world map puzzle, and the others write letters to an adopted "grandteacher" who is a pen-pal for the students.

Once a week, the teacher from the "nearby" Fence Creek School drives one hour to spend a day at Hanging Woman with her entire student body: one twelve-year-old boy. Debbie Worman lives in a trailer on Ryan Bulkley's family ranch, where her job is to teach Ryan, who would spend up to three hours a day on a bus if it weren't for the school on his ranch. Their trips to Hanging Woman are a good break from seeing only each other. Ryan will travel 72 miles over very muddy, rutted and untrustworthy spring roads to take his Student Achievement Tests in Clearmont. And he goes with the Hanging Woman students to Clearmont twice a month for art classes, computer training, and use of the library.

For physical education, Ryan and Debbie take a walk. He has taught her to play chess, she has helped his mother deliver a calf. And when spring storms cut power to their school, they simply moved up to Ryan's home for four days and studied beside the wood-burning stove.

Robert Phinney has to be creative to teach the same subject areas to children who range in age from five to ten years old.

A woman named Mabel in a town called Jay Em gave us a tour of her unlikely retirement spot.

Her neighbor, Russell Spahr, said, "I came from Indiana and retired to San Diego, but when I crossed the state line into Wyoming, I told my wife I felt at home for the first time in my life." It took him 62 years to find home.

"I came in 1918, and feel the same way," Mabel told him.

"And here, all along, I thought you were a native," he chuckled. It's true that to some in Wyoming, living in the state for 72 years after being born somewhere else isn't the same as really being from here.

Jay Em is an idyllic spot, green for Wyoming, on a creek 17 miles from Lusk. It was not named for the man who built the town and whose life inspires stories and whispered rumors that still are murmured in the near-ghost town. No, the name was for Jim Moore, an early cattle rancher whose brand was a "J" and rolling "M."

But it's a man named Lake Harris whose body was carried over the creek on a bridge built just for the occasion to lay beside his two wives in the stone crypt in Jay Em's cemetery. And it was Lake who, apparently boiling over with energy, built the general store, the lumber mill, the feed supply store, a factory producing tombstones and fireplace facings from local granite, a striking granite church, a wishing well beside the bank, and a moat beside his house.

Lake outlived a first wife who died in the flu epidemic of 1918. And he watched helplessly as his second wife was trampled by a cow known to dislike women. His wife had just stepped out of the car to stretch her legs when the murderous mother cow knocked her down and stomped her to death. They say Lake was odd after that.

Sheep ribbon roping is a team event at the annual Sheepherder's Fair in tiny Powder River. One person ropes the sheep, then the other grabs the ribbon that's tied to the animal's tail.

Once she has the ribbon, the contestant races to the other end of the arena, trying to set a winning time. Often, it's a father-daughter event, although sometimes boyfriends and girlfriends are a team.

Teenagers relax outside the Quonset hut where lamb dishes are judged, wool creations are sold, and ranchers socialize at the Sheepherder's Fair.

Dogs are the star competitors. Border collies trained in herding have a tough task
—they're supposed to chase six ewes through a narrow passage between two fences
into a pen. Trainers use verbal or hand signals to help the dog's strategy.
The winning time in this event was under two minutes.

The Master of Ceremonies handles a variety of events. Some celebrate tough ranch skills. Others are silly, such as the event where a ribbon is tied to the ewe's tail, and a contestant has to grab it and race to the end of the field.

The top rodeo stars earn six figure salaries. But on the entry level, it's a life spent more in trucks than on bucking broncs. One retired bull rider said it wasn't the broken bones that got to him, but the trips to a different rodeo every night, trying to win $20 or $30, "just enough to pay for the gas."

"You know what to do, buddy," says the rodeo clown to his friend, about to jump on an angry bull. The clown is a crucial partner in the action. He'll put himself in harm's way, distracting the bull, so the fallen rider can get out of the arena. It was one of this teenager's first professional rides. Competitors in this little arena behind a bar are mostly ranch kids trying to become professionals.

*Traditional-style polo is played near Sheridan on summer Sundays. It's not as out
of place in Wyoming as it seems. British investors were active in establishing cattle
ranching in the area, and their influence remains in this horse country. On one
of her trips to the U.S., Queen Elizabeth of Great Britain stayed on the ranch
owned by Senator Malcolm Wallop's family, where the oldest polo field in the
country was located.*

There's also "Cowboy Polo." In this version, each team has four players and the riders use a broom and ball. But both styles are a rough contact sport, hard on the horses and the riders. At the Cody "Centennial Ranch Roundup", other events were Wild Cow Milking, Mutton Bustin (children riding sheep), and Ranch Branding.

Wyoming is a good place to break into rodeo. A fledgling bronc rider or rodeo clown can get experience by traveling around the state to the little community competitions, then move up to the "big time" events, such as the Central Wyoming Fair and Rodeo.

*Watching the bull riding at the
fairgrounds in Casper*

Saturday night at the Merc, in Atlantic City. The bar was a fixture for gold miners a century ago, and a getaway spot now for Wyoming people fond of the historic, nearly abandoned town.

Country swing dancing at Cassie's Supper Club in Cody.

Western states have to warn drivers when they're entering a "no services" stretch. It's not something a Japanese, European, or East Coast person could be expected to anticipate. But in the West, half a gas tank may not get you to the next town. And there won't be a farmhouse or pay phone to call from when you run out of gas. In a state with more antelope than service stations, there are plenty of lonely roads.

Floyd Widmer lives on the road from Casper to Shoshoni, a hundred miles to the northwest. His town is Waltman, population 10, according to the road sign, but really just three live there now. To the west is a rest stop, then another town with a handful of people, Hiland. East is Powder River, where the population is big enough (at 50) that you have to slow down for the 45-second drive through town. Standing in his dusty driveway, Floyd sees the tops of hills to the south, and bare land with sagebrush in all other directions.

Floyd and his wife, Sharon, own the Waltman Store, but he's best known for the car collection out back.

"Bought 60 at a time one year," says Floyd, and he thinks he got a good deal. "Twenty-eight dollars apiece at the Casper City pound auction. But you have to take them all. Got 60 or 70. Them's the back rows over there." Floyd looks as dusty and used as his vehicles, but he has human qualities they lack, his smile being the best. It's sheepish, but with a hint of the wolf in it. Both calm victim, and crafty predator.

His life is as populated as his road is empty. To start with the obvious, there's Sharon and the son who lives at home. Floyd and Sharon have raised eleven children, only about half of them at the Waltman Store.

"The most we've had steady on is seven," he says.

But the Waltman Store is home to more than family. Every day, except for Sunday, Sharon cooks for anybody who's hungry. It's not necessarily required that they pay.

'If we had money for ever penny written here (on her bulletin board of IOU's), we could go to Hawaii for a month."

"A year," says her husband.

Along a road where antelope outnumber the cars, sits the Waltman Store. For twenty years, Floyd and Sharon Widmer have ministered to travelers on the 100-mile stretch between Casper and Shoshoni. Customers say Sharon's burgers are "the best in the world," and Floyd can fix anything wrong with a car. The conversation isn't too bad, either.

"But two fellas, this beats it, come here for hamburgers cause they heard from the roadworkers that mine are the best in the world. They eat, and drink three beers each, and leave. "Bout two hours later, back they come. They drove 60 miles and remembered they didn't pay, so back they come."

They won't need to come back to pay for beer by next year, if Sharon makes good on her threat. "Alcohol, Tobacca and Firearms wrote me," she says, meaning the federal agency. "There's a tax on sellin' booze they say I haven't paid in twelve years. Plus interest—it's eleven-hundirt dollars. I don't need to sell the damned beer. It's just for folks that wants it with their hamburger. Or th' highway girls take a six-pack with them. Same with th' guys at the mine."

The letter about this tax sounds defensive, not exactly what you'd expect from a federal agency. Still, it says people should have known about the tax. It said they put notices in trade journals about it.

Trade journals! "What kind of trade journals would you be in?" I ask. "The Trade Journal of Little Stores with Some of Whatever You Don't Want to Buy?" The Waltman Store has an old-fashioned general store selection: knives, pickled eggs, and soap next to oven mitts and little flowered goose outfits for a teapot, made by a lady in Powder River. In the middle is the CB radio with Highway Patrol and Sheriff's calls drifting through the static. Another service of the Waltman Store is arriving first at the scene of car wrecks, rollovers, and flat tires. Floyd's son has a collection of pictures of these.

Good-natured kidding is the dominant mood at the cafe, which never emptied the entire day I sat there. In the corner, a patron named Ray replied to my question, "'Naw—the Trade Journal of Good Burgers, Bad Garage Sale Stuff, and Junk."

(He meant Floyd's nearly two thousand cars, the old Waltman Train depot, a milk truck, and the pile of torn-down utility poles. All this was purchased by Floyd and stacked as neatly as rusting metal objects can be, behind the cafe on land Floyd thinks must be "poisoned. I never can grow trees."

Everybody liked Ray's insult except Floyd, who said, "You want junk—go over th' next hill and look at that junk. People want to buy what I've got here. Guy and his two sons asked me yesterday if they could just look at the old cars. Guy offered to buy those poles, but I told him no. I had in my mind I'd fence in, but like lots of things, I never did."

Floyd Widmer's love of cars and trucks is not an unusual attitude in Wyoming. More vehicles are registered in the state than there are people. Trucks and trailers account for nearly half of the registered vehicles. Visitors drop by the "collection" behind the Waltman Cafe to admire the antiques.

The trade journal letter got everyone going. Elsie is Sharon's partner in garage-sale search missions. She sat at the counter in tight, white jeans, and a belt with "E-L-S-I-E" written on it. She told Ray, eating eggs in the corner, "You should of come down to that ranch auction Sunday. That's where Sharon got th' flowers over in the milk can. You heard of that old lady that owned the ranch? She had taste. Nice stuff." The flowers were paper. They were huge, and maybe the sun had faded them. Their colors were watery green, pink, and red.

"I wouldn't wipe Pete's paws with those flowers," said Ray. Pete is a dog. He got up at the mention of his name and walked over to gaze hopefully at Ray's eggs.

"You watch, somebody'll buy 'em," said Sharon. "I just hope they pay 11 hundirt for 'em in time to pay this bill."

If the beer goes, it'll be the second casualty of the government at the Waltman Store. Floyd dug up his gas tanks earlier this spring. Laws on leaking underground storage tanks drove Floyd out of that business. "You talk to the lady in Natrona (pop., 5)? She stopped sellin' gas last weekend. Now the only place to stop between Casper and Shoshoni is Hiland."

Over the past 20 years, selling gas has earned Floyd and Sharon 42 thousand dollars, total.

Floyd says cutting out gas sales doesn't matter too much. It's the grocery business he minds losing. "We sold a lot of groceries, but when the cars got better and the roads got better, they started goin' to town."

"Hey Floyd," said Ray. "Pretty soon all you'll have for sale here is dumb paper flowers and hamburger grease. You'll be just like old Pete. You'll have to steal people to come here." Floyd's son has pictures he says prove that Pete has stolen kittens and brought them home to play with. In one photo, the dog is asleep with his paw over a kitten, curled up next to him.

Floyd grinned his sly grin, and his sheep eyes looked out from under the brim of his cap. "Naw, Ray, you'd keep comin' here if you had to eat pickled eggs ever' meal. You just like the company."

Floyd was right.

Powder River, the biggest town (pop. 50) on the road from Casper to Shoshoni.

Susan Anderson was born in Pittsburgh, Pennsylvania. She has a B.A. from the College of Wooster and an M.S. from the Columbia University Graduate School of Journalism.

Her broadcast journalism career includes freelance photography in New York; writing at WCBS Radio in New York; and writing, producing, and reporting at KGO Television and KPIX Television in San Francisco. She received two Emmies for writing and producing a documentary on Cuba for Westinghouse Broadcasting in 1977. Since moving to Wyoming in 1980, she has been a reporter and News Director at KTWO Television and Radio in Casper, where she has won awards for reporting from the Wyoming Association of Broadcasters, and Associated Press.

She has also been a reporter at the Casper Star-Tribune, and freelance contributor to Wyoming 100, a centennial magazine published by the Casper Star-Tribune.

PHOTOS / JACEK BOGUCKI

Zbigniew Bzdak was born in Radomsko, Poland. He studied in Cracow, with a major in nuclear physics, chemistry, and electronics. Bzdak's photography has been published widely since he settled in the United States in 1980. His work has appeared in National Geographic, Outside, Americas, Reader's Digest, Outdoor Photographer, and in numerous books and newspapers.

He has been news photographer and editor for two Casper, Wyoming, television stations, and now is chief photographer at the Casper Star-Tribune. In addition, Bzdak was the photographer for the Canoandes Expedition (1979-82), which explored and documented Latin American white-water rivers.

He was also the photographer for, and a member of, the first exploration team to successfully navigate the entire length of the Amazon River in 1985-86. His photographs for the expedition were published by National Geographic, Outside, and Alfred A. Knopf.

Bzdak became an American citizen in 1988.